CW00347249

HAUNTED
LIVERPOOL

VOLUME FOUR

© Tom Slemen 2008

Published by The Bluecoat Press, Liverpool
Book design by March Graphic Design Studio, Liverpool
Cover illustration by Tim Webster
Printed by Grafo

ISBN 9781904438748

All rights reserved. No part of this publication may be reproduced, stored in a
retrieval system, or transmitted in any form or by any means, electronic, mechanical,
photocopying, recording or otherwise, without prior permission from the publisher.

THE BLUECOAT PRESS
3 Brick Street
Liverpool L1 0BL

Telephone 0151 707 2390
Website www.bluecoatpress.co.uk

Front cover *The Werewolves of County Fermanagh*, page 86

TOM SLEMEN

HAUNTED LIVERPOOL

VOLUME FOUR

THE BLUECOAT PRESS

Contents

BORN TOO LATE

Love can transcend almost any obstacle. It can leapfrog over age differences, see beyond the colour of a person's skin and bridge the gulf between rich and poor. The following story, which happened a long time ago, seems to indicate that love can even transcend time itself.

On a snowy Saturday afternoon in December 1901, Rose Mooney sat basking in front of a blazing log fire in the caretaker's quarters at Speke Hall; a beautiful, half-timbered Tudor mansion in south Liverpool. Her husband, Desmond, looked after the hall with the help of a few gardeners and a stableman. On this wintry afternoon, he was in a pub in town, enjoying a drink with a relative, so Mrs Mooney's only company was her eleven-year-old daughter Maude, a fresh-faced girl with long, deep auburn hair that she usually wore in two pony-tails. Mrs Mooney was five months pregnant and Maude was looking forward to having a baby brother or sister to look after.

Maude went out to play in the hall's beautifully-kept grounds, as she did most days. Sometimes her cousin or a friend from school joined her, but being December and close to Christmas, all her friends were with their families. Maude decided to build a snowman and borrowed her father's old fishing hat to put on top of his big round head. At around four o'clock, twilight started to creep across the sky, so Mrs Mooney pulled on a coat and went to shout for her daughter. There was not a sound in the silent frosty garden and no sign of Maude. When Mr Mooney returned home, he too joined in the search.

The worried pair followed the trail of footsteps leading from the snowman on the front lawn, for over two hundred yards, then stopped abruptly. Next to the impressions of Maude's shoes were some other footsteps, slightly larger than Maude's and had made by shoes with a heel. The mystery deepened when the Mooneys discovered that both sets of footprints came to a full stop near two ancient sprawling yew trees, known as 'Adam and Eve'.

The gardener, George, came wheezing across the lawn and added another puzzle to the unfolding mystery. He had seen Maude throwing snowballs at what looked like a little girl in a large floppy hat. Mr Mooney interrupted him, "No, George, that must have been the snowman, with my hat on." The gardener shook his head and insisted that a young girl, dressed in a peculiar black costume, had been playing with her. She had certainly not been a snowman by any stretch of the imagination. This new piece of information upset Mrs Mooney, "Where can she be?" she sobbed, as her equally distraught husband tried to comfort her.

"Don't worry, my love, I'm sure all will be well," he said, trying to mask his own anxiety. Then, turning to George, he said, "Take Mrs Mooney back to the house. I'm just going to find out where Maude's hiding." Then, under his breath, he added, "I'm going to call the police."

Moments later, before George could do as he was asked, the sound of a child laughing could be heard coming from the trees. It was Maude's laughter and the lost child suddenly came skipping across the snow-covered lawns, wearing a little cape of some sort. Her relieved parents and the gardener closed in on her and as her mother sobbed and hugged her, Maude's father chided her and demanded to know where she had been. Maude's mood immediately changed. She dropped her head in a sulk and her bottom lip quivered. "I'm not to say. It's a secret," she muttered.

"Secret? I'll give you a good hiding, my girl, never mind

secret. Now tell us where you've been. Your mother and I have been worried sick."

"Stop it, Desmond. She's here, that's all that matters. She'll tell us in her own time. Now let's get her inside before we all freeze to death!" Rose Mooney, like any mother who has briefly faced the possibility of harm coming to her child, gratefully squeezed her daughter in her arms and led her indoors.

Despite her father's anger and frustration, Maude could not be persuaded to say where she had been that afternoon. Desmond Mooney examined the little black cloak she had on. It was beautifully made of luxurious black velvet with a dark violet silk lining, decorated with a border of gold stitching. There were no labels to indicate who had made it, or its owner's name.

On many more occasions, up until August of the following year, Maude would vanish for hours on end, and her parents and many other people visiting the hall were witness to the strange disappearances. Sometimes, another girl's voice and laughter could be heard, though she could not be seen. On such occasions the gardener's old English sheepdog used to act strangely, and seemed able to discern things in the grounds that humans could not. In the end, Desmond Mooney secured a new job in Ormskirk, and he and his family moved away from Speke Hall. Maude Mooney cried her eyes out when they moved, as if she felt so intensely for her invisible playmate that she could not bear to part from him or her.

In 1911, when she reached the age of twenty-one, Maude finally broke her silence, and told her mother about the supernatural goings-on at Speke Hall. She described how she had fallen in love with a little Cavalier boy named Tristam. He had lived hundreds of years ago, but could somehow occasionally visit the present. How this had been possible Maude could not say, but what she did know was that she had loved Tristam and he had returned her love. They would walk hand in hand through the grounds, laughing and playing, and she had even met his parents and their servants at the hall. They rode on Tristam's horse along the banks of the Mersey and kissed under one of the old yew trees. He had often given her roses and serenaded her with an instrument like a guitar and had even given her his cape when Maude was shivering with cold that December afternoon when they first met and they had carved their initials into the bark of a tree.

The identity of Tristam has not been established as yet. It is said that in 1969, when Maude was a frail old woman, she asked to be taken to Speke Hall, where she passed away on a bright sunny afternoon, aged seventy-nine. Perhaps she has been reunited with Tristam for good now.

CHANGE OF HEART

In the mid-1950s, in Liverpool, a man named Leo Burns lost his wife. She died as she was undergoing an operation, and she was only thirty-two. Leo was devastated by her untimely death, and like many men in such a position, he turned to drink. Within six months, he had lost his job and virtually all his friends. Sinking deeper and deeper into depression, he was eventually evicted for non-payment of rent and ended up as a vagrant.

The only real friend Leo had was an elderly priest who urged him to stop wallowing in self pity. The priest repeatedly encouraged Leo to get a job and to get his life back on track, but he continued to drink; he just could not see any light. He would beg and steal to get enough money for a bottle of gin or whisky, and often cadged food at the home for vagrants on Shaw Street.

In the bitter winter of December 1956, Leo struggled to sleep on a park bench wrapped in newspapers, but it was no good; the biting cold cut through the paper and his filthy, tattered clothes, gnawing at his bones. He trudged out of the park blowing his fingers, then thrusting them inside his coat pockets to try and get some sensation back. He was lucky enough to be given a bunk at a home for the destitute on Brownlow Hill, but had to leave after stealing another person's suit while he was asleep. Determined not to freeze to death under the stars, he devised a desperate plan to get good food and shelter. He picked up a brick from a back alley and hurled it through a jeweller's window on Mount Pleasant, knowing it would not be long before the police turned up to arrest him. They would take him to Walton Jail, where he would be given a delicious Christmas dinner.

Three policemen duly did turn up, and Leo stood on the pavement by the smashed window, ready to be handcuffed, but instead they ran past him and chased an innocent man trotting after a bus by the Adelphi Hotel. "It was me, you idiots! Me!" he yelled after them. The jeweller swore at Leo and told him to beat it.

With the temperature still dropping and a freezing wind whistling straight off the Mersey, Leo quickly devised another plan to get himself arrested and taken off the wintry streets. He walked into a restaurant on Bold Street which he and his wife used to frequent, wearing the stolen suit. A waiter escorted him to a table and offered him the menu. Before Leo made his choices, he asked for a cigar, which the restaurant offered freely to customers as a courtesy. He ordered the best wine, then, after studying the menu for some time – he was in no rush – he decided to sample a few exotic dishes, including duck, with dessert to follow. He would enjoy his meal, and the cosy, warm surroundings, before declaring himself insolvent. Once the proprietors found out that he could not pay the bill, they were bound to call the police who would lock him up. That would earn him a few warm nights in Cheapside, or Walton, just in time for the Christmas dinner.

Once again though, his criminal intentions backfired. Leo asked for the bill, read the amount due, then leaned back on the chair, puffing on the cigar. "Can't pay I'm afraid," he smirked. "I'm stony broke."

The waiter turned red with anger, then signalled to a colleague, who kept the door covered in case Leo attempted to make a run for it. The manager was summoned; a small fat man, with a curly mop of silvery hair, he emerged from the back of the restaurant. When he saw Leo, he reacted as if he had seen a ghost – as it turned out, the ghost of a much missed person. His face drained of colour and became expressionless. "Daniel, is that … you?" he asked.

Leo was baffled; this was not the expected reaction. His plan was going wrong again. "Pardon?" he asked.

The Jewish restaurant owner muttered something in Hebrew, as tears began rolling down his face. He stared intently at Leo, scrutinising each of his features in turn. The two waiters did not know what to make of it. The proprietor then told Leo that he was the exact double of his younger brother Daniel, who had died in a German concentration camp in World War Two and he reached out and grabbed his hand, squeezing it hard. When the waiters tried to tell him that Leo was just a penniless bum, the old man ignored them and Leo was let off without any punishment. The restaurant owner apologised to his customers as he wiped away the tears.

When Leo Burns thought about the fate of his double in Auschwitz, he finally saw the light. Nothing he had gone through was as bad the horrors suffered in the concentration camps. This stark realisation quickly helped him pull himself together, and within weeks he had found a job, and though it was a long battle, he finally kicked his drink habit. I suppose the moral of this story is that, however bad things may seem, there is always someone worse off than oneself.

GHOST OF CLAYTON SQUARE

In February 2000, thirty-year-old Adam from Speke, left the Virgin Megastore in town with his friend Tony. The day was Monday, 14 February, Valentine's Day, and Adam's girlfriend Allison had asked him to buy a romantic video and a little gift for her. Nothing extravagant, just a little thing that would mean a lot. He searched the shelves but could not find a suitable video. Tony, getting increasingly bored, suggested *Last Tango In Paris*, but Adam said there was nothing romantic about the film. So they wandered off into Clayton Square Shopping Centre and found themselves outside the Body Shop. "Do us a favour, Tony," Adam said. "I get really flustered when I go in shops like this. Get me a basket of smellies, will you? I'll buy you a pint."

"No way! You must be joking! I'm not doing your dirty work for you."

"Ah! Go on, Tony. I won't have anything to give to Allison … and I promised."

"You need to get a grip, mate. That Allison's got you round her little finger. She's turning you into a middle-aged bore. You never go to the match any more and what's happened to our Saturday night benders?"

"But me and Allison are saving ..." Adam began.

"Leave it out, Adam. You can stuff your smellies and your romantic videos. I'm off," snarled Tony.

He marched off angrily, leaving Adam lingering outside the Body Shop. A voice from behind greeted him. The stranger was about twenty at the most, and had a mullet hairstyle with a feathered fringe and a parting down the middle of his head. He wore a black V-necked pullover on which there was a logo of a pouncing cat, and underneath, the word 'Slazenger'. His jeans were baggy at the top, but tapered inwards as they went down to his Gola trainers. Adam nodded back, then walked into the Body Shop to get away from the out-dated looking youth, but he followed him inside saying, "I used to go with Allison Jones."

"What?" asked Adam, swinging round to face him.

"I saw you with her in the precinct the other day. She hasn't changed much."

"Oh, I'll tell her. What's your name?" he responded unenthusiastically.

"Paul. Say Paul from High Park Street. Tell her I was asking," the youth replied.

"When were you seeing her?" Adam asked, uncomfortable with the conversation.

Paul said it was when she was thirteen till she was fifteen. As she was now twenty-six, it was a long time ago. Yet this dubious character seemed to know everything about her.

Then Adam had what he thought was a bright idea. He asked Paul if he would go into the Body Shop and buy a gift for Allison, confiding that he had a hang up about buying feminine things. Paul was amenable and went into the store, soon re-emerging with a basketful of lotions and creams. "Thanks, mate," said Adam. "Say, how come you're not buying your girl something? It's Valentine's Day you know."

Paul seemed choked up all of a sudden and his eyes became watery, but simply shrugged and said nothing. Adam suspected he was single, and had probably just come out of a relationship. He felt awkward, realising his lack of tact. Trying to lighten the mood, he laughed and said, "She wanted me to get her a romantic video, but I couldn't find one. I was thinking of getting her a 'Forever Friends' teddy, a big one. You could go in and get it for me if you want."

"She used to have a cabbage patch doll called Trudy," said Paul, mournfully.

"Wait till I tell her all this, she'll be dead embarrassed," giggled Adam. "Trudy!"

"I remember there were two films she loved. One was ET," Paul suggested.

"That's years old," Adam frowned.

"When ET used to say 'bee gooood', then point to his heart and say, 'I'll be right here,' she always used to cry."

Unconvinced, Adam said, "Nah, she's seen that film about fifty times. What was the other video she liked?"

"An old black and white film called A Guy Named Joe. It was about a pilot from the Second World War who died, but he comes back from heaven to help the boyfriend of the girl he left behind."

"I'm not getting her a black and white film, she'd go bananas," said Adam, not picking up the connection.

All of a sudden, he noticed that Paul was crying silently. Before he could ask what was wrong, the youth had walked away. He vanished round a corner and never returned. Adam searched for him but could not find him anywhere.

When Adam went home to Allison, he told her about Paul from High Park Street, and she seemed to be deeply shocked. She said he could not possibly have chatted with him, because he had been killed in a car crash in Widnes years ago – on Valentine's Day. Adam's gulped when she told him this. She even produced an old photograph of Paul; without question the same person he had spoken to in Clayton Square. Allison admitted that she did once have a cabbage patch doll named Trudy, and yes, she always cried at the end of *ET*. She also recalled that in her teenage days, her favourite romantic film had been *A Guy Named Joe*, so Adam managed to get hold of a copy and cradled an emotional Allison in his arms as they watched it.

BUT FOR THE GRACE OF GOD

One evening in July 1999, Derek, a middle-aged businessman from Knowsley, was in Bold Street with Tony, a friend from work. As they were passing a shop doorway, a beggar held out a grimy hand and asked, "Could you spare any change please, lads?" Without giving him a second glance, Derek said something which ended with the word 'off' and walked on. Tony, however, stopped and gave the man some money. "You shouldn't encourage them, mate," said Derek, eyeing the hunched figure with pure contempt.

"Remember that old saying, Derek, 'There but for the grace of God go I.'" And then, turning to the beggar, Tony said, "Just ignore him. Go and get yourself some hot food."

Derek shook his head in disbelief and the two of them walked on to a club.

The next day, in Knowsley, a *Big Issue* seller asked them if they would like to buy a copy. Tony said he already had that week's issue and walked on, but Derek reached into his inside pocket. The vendor thought he was getting out his wallet and started to fold up the magazine for him. Instead, he got out a folded up document and handed it to the homeless man with a sneer. "Here, this is a housing benefit form. Fill it in and you won't be homeless anymore."

"For God's sake, Derek, stop messing about."

The *Big Issue* seller muttered, "Have a nice day, sir," and despondently unfolded the top copy of his pile.

Derek smirked, thinking he had made a really clever joke. However, that night, at ten minutes to eleven, that smirk was wiped off his face. He had rung for a taxi and was leaving the Derby Arms on Knowsley Lane. As he came out of the pub there was the beggar he had insulted the day before, standing in the shadows. Derek recognised him immediately. The taxi turned up and Derek jumped inside.

"That beggar's weird, isn't he?" he said to the cabby, clicking his seat belt on.

"Which beggar?" said the cabby, checking his mirrors and looking around. The beggar was no longer anywhere to be seen.

On the following day, at 5pm, Derek was in Liverpool city centre, shopping with his girlfriend, Jenni. They had parked their car at the bottom of Brownlow Hill, and as they were heading back to the car park, he suddenly made an unplanned detour up Bold Street. When Jenni asked him why, he said he wanted to see if the beggar was sitting in his usual doorway, because he wanted to ask him what he had been doing up near the Derby Arms.

"Oh let it go, Derek," said Jenni, pulling on his arm. "My feet are killing me and I'm dying for a cuppa."

But he was determined to find the beggar. However, when he got to the Bold Street doorway, he saw something which sent an unpleasant shiver down his spine. The grubby-looking man slumped dejectedly in the doorway, with his stubbled face and greasy hair, was an exact double of himself. Jenni was speechless and Derek just stood there, gaping at the unfortunate man. He had a small but distinctive mole on his left cheek, and so did the beggar. It was not as if this man was just a look-alike. He *was* Derek. The strange thing was that the doppelganger never once looked at him, but kept his eyes fixed on the pavement with a slight grin playing on his face.

Derek and Jenni hurried away from him without exchanging a word, but when they reached the car park, and were safely back inside their car, they went over and over what they had just witnessed, but could make no sense of it.

This inexplicable event took place in 1999, and Derek and Jenni still refuse to venture anywhere near Bold Street.

TERROR ON THE M62

The following incident was related to me in September 2001, by a well-known Liverpool comedian whom I cannot identify. He stipulated that he would only relate the full facts if I would give him my word that I would never identify him. I shall therefore have to call him 'Bob'.

In the early 1990s, Bob drove up the M62 to Manchester, where he was due to perform a comedy routine as part of a cabaret show. As usual, his performance was very warmly received by the audience, and, in appreciation, he decided to go back onstage for a further twenty minutes. While performing his additional material, he noticed a beautiful young woman sitting at a table smiling at him. She reminded him of the Seventies film star, Farrah Fawcett Majors. After he had finished his act and had basked in the audience's enthusiastic applause for a while, Bob went backstage and changed, before being escorted by the manager to a specially-reserved table for a meal and drink.

Just before the next performer took to the stage, Bob

made his way over to the table where the woman was sitting alone and asked if she would care to join him. She smiled, and accepted without any hesitation. She was very tall and looked even more attractive at close quarters, with her sapphire-blue eyes and long blonde hair. In a soft voice, she introduced herself as Danielle. Her accent was not local and was difficult to place.

Bob ordered champagne and was soon flirting with Danielle. She, however, refused the champagne, preferring to sip mineral water. There was a 'stay-behind' at the club, and it was not long before Bob and Danielle were embracing on the dance floor. He learned that the reason she was on her own was that her boyfriend had arranged to meet her at the club, but had not turned up for some reason. She told him that she lived in St Helens, and Bob suggested that, as she had not been drinking, she could drive him home to Merseyside in his car. She was not keen and instead suggested that Bob stay overnight at her home until he was fit enough to drive in the morning.

At 3am, they left the Manchester club and walked through the chilly night air towards the car park. Danielle shivered in her sleeveless top, so Bob gave her his leather jacket. After strapping Bob's seatbelt on for him because he was so intoxicated, they embarked on the return journey down the M62. Bob fumbled with the radio controls, but Danielle's hand intercepted his, and so they sat in silence as the car sped along the motorway.

Suddenly stirring from his alcohol-induced doze, Bob turned to look at Danielle and saw something that still gives him nightmares to this day. Her beautiful features had contorted into what can only be described as a demonic scowl. Her head swivelled towards him and her eyes turned blood red, as her mouth opened wide – twice as wide as a normal mouth – to reveal a fearsome array of pointed teeth.

The comedian instantly sobered up, but felt faint and breathless. She must be some sort of supernatural entity and was driving him goodness knows where. As if able to read his mind, the thing in the driving seat shrieked with manic laughter and zig-zagged suicidally between lanes. Bob was not religious, but found himself imploring Jesus to save him. The car suddenly screeched into a 180-degree turn and careered off the hard shoulder on to a slip road, then veered into a ditch. Bob tried to get out, but in his blind panic, he forgot to unclick his seatbelt. He screamed out for help, his mind in turmoil, and looked back in terror at the seat beside him – empty, except for his jacket, with no trace of the fiend masquerading as a woman.

The police found him wandering along the hard shoulder. His bizarre tale was not believed. The management at the club confirmed that he had left with a woman at the wheel of his own car, but no one at the club had any idea who 'Danielle' was. Bob was badly shaken by the incident and has never appeared at the Manchester club since.

THE HIGHEST JUDGE

In December 1893, at Columbia, Mississippi, two hundred people threw their hats into the air and cheered, as festivities commenced and the saloons dispensed free drinks. The despicable cause of the celebrations was the lynching of a young black man, who had allegedly raped a farmer's fifteen-year-old daughter. The sheriff more or less turned a blind eye to the lynching, for he himself was suspected of being a member of the local branch of the Ku Klux Klan, who were responsible for the lynching.

A fortnight later, in an almost copycat incident, another woman was raped at knifepoint by a masked man, in front of her children. The traumatised victim told the sheriff's men that the attacker was definitely white, because she had glimpsed his bare hands and parts of his face. Nevertheless, another black youth was targeted by the racist mob, but luckily he caught wind of what was going on and escaped by fleeing the town. The frustrated lynch mob, seeking vengeance, burned down his family's home.

Around this time, preacher Joseph Levine came to town and was appalled and sickened by the bigotry, lynchings and kangaroo courts he found there. He had emigrated to America from Sefton, Lancashire, three years before, after experiencing a religious vision. Levine once burst into a saloon in Columbia, leapt on to a table, and spontaneously delivered a sermon. He declared that God was the highest judge of all and that the state of a man's soul was the only thing that mattered – the colour of his skin was of absolutely no importance. Heckled and booed, he persevered with his message. Then one rowdy citizen fetched a bullwhip and tried to strike the preacher, but as he drew back the whip, it lashed out the eye of his own son. This enraged the crowd even more and Levine was lucky to escape with his life. A local widow gave him refuge, but said he would soon have to leave, otherwise the mob would destroy her home for sheltering a man who sympathised with the black folk.

On 7 February of that year, a young white man, Will Purvis, was taken to the town's gallows to be hanged for the murder of a farmer in Columbia, despite wide rumours that a man named Joe Beard had actually killed the farmer, so the preacher intervened. The 3,000-strong crowd spat and threw stones at him as he managed to climb on to the platform supporting the gallows. The hangman had already placed the noose around Will Purvis's neck and tied his hands behind his back. The sheriff, Irvin Magee, and his deputy, grabbed the preacher and held him firmly. They turned Levine towards Purvis. "You can watch him die, preacherman," sneered the deputy.

Joseph Levine suddenly cried out, "I call upon the Highest Judge of all to halt this injustice. I call upon the Lord my God!"

The trapdoor snapped open, and the condemned man was plunging to his doom, when, suddenly, the noose came undone and slid over his head. Purvis landed on his feet below the stage, then crumpled in a heap. The hangman examined the dangling rope, completely mystified. The people in the crowd had gasped as one, and then watched, silent and tense, seeming to regard the freak incident as a miracle. The sheriff nervously announced that the rope had been made of grass which had been too wiry to keep a knot. Will Purvis was led back on to the gallows and a new noose was made and placed over his head. Something strange then took place that has never been explained to this day.

The people in the front rows began gabbling in an unknown language. It sounded like complete gibberish. Many thought they were speaking in tongues – a well reported phenomenon during outbreaks of religious mania. The townsfolk surged towards the stage and demanded that the sheriff reprieve Purvis. He refused at first but, intimidated by the angry, babbling mob, he had to bend to their wishes.

Purvis was re-tried and found guilty, but friends and supporters attacked the prison and managed to free him. Still professing his innocence, he later surrendered and his death sentence was commuted to life imprisonment. The jurors who had found him guilty had been twelve notorious members of the lynching party. At the trial, the distraught Purvis ominously warned the jurors that he would live to see the last one of them die.

Several years later, the real killer, Joe Beard, confessed on his deathbed to the farmer's murder, and Will Purvis was exonerated and set free. Oddly, every one of the jurors who had wrongly sentenced him died, one after another, so Purvis did indeed outlive them, just as he had predicted. The rope that miraculously unknotted itself has since been analysed many times but no defect could be found. To his dying day, Will Purvis believed that God had intervened to save him.

GRIDLOCK

Many foolish things have been done in an attempt to win a woman's heart, and the following is an extreme example.

In 1811, in the luxurious setting of the new Exchange Coffee Rooms, in Liverpool, two businessmen, both aged fifty-five, were having a discussion about who they thought was the most beautiful woman in the city. Daniel Doyle insisted that a young lady named Henrietta Shelbourne was the finest creature he had ever set eyes upon, and his friend Nathan Kingsley was forced to agree. Mr Doyle bemoaned the fact that he and his bachelor friend had to resign themselves to the fact that they were far too old for Miss Shelbourne, who had just turned twenty-one, but his friend disagreed. Mr Doyle sighed, then sank back deep in thought as he puffed thoughtfully on his pipe. After a time, he announced, "I have heard that Henrietta will be attending a ball at Colonel Denney's, in Belgravia, on Sunday."

"Really?" replied Kingsley with a dreamy smile.

The two men decided to attend the ball, just to be in the presence of the delightful Miss Shelbourne, so they boarded the train for London. During the journey, Daniel Doyle drank too much whisky, and foolishly bet his friend a thousand guineas that he could win Miss Shelbourne's heart. Mr Kingsley readily accepted the wager.

The lovesick pair attended the ball, and when they set eyes on Henrietta, they both felt instantly rejuvenated. She looked stunningly beautiful in a sparkling, sequinned, sky-blue dress, surrounded by a flock of admirers, as usual. She was something of a wit, which was part of her charisma and brought men flocking to her side.

As the night wore on, Daniel Doyle saw his opportunity when he engineered the chance of a dance with Henrietta. He was thoroughly intoxicated, both with whisky and with love, and passionately beseeched the lady of his dreams, "What must a man do to win your heart?"

Henrietta threw back her head, smiling broadly, and replied, "He must make me feel like the most special thing in the world." Then she giggled coquettishly, and pressed her nose against his. "Bring London to a standstill for me," she whispered in his ear. Her face was pressed so close, that Mr Doyle felt her fluttering eyelashes against his cheek. It was as though an electric shock had coursed through his veins. Her powerful rose-perfumed scent dizzied his brain, more powerfully than any drug. Henrietta then pulled herself free from his embrace and three much younger men simultaneously approached for the prospect of a dance.

After the ball, Daniel Doyle asked Henrietta where she was staying, and she told him she would be in London for just one week, at her uncle's house near Shaftsbury Avenue.

"Within three days I shall bring London to a standstill for

you. If I succeed, will I have won your heart?" he asked.

"Perhaps," she smirked, then lifted her knuckles to Daniel's lips and he gently kissed them.

Henrietta was then escorted home by her uncle, as every man in the room sighed and every young woman breathed a sigh of relief. Nathan Kingsley, seeing that his friend was besotted by Miss Shelbourne, generously offered to forget the wager. And so the bet was cancelled.

The two admirers then booked into a hotel overlooking Shaftsbury Avenue. The next day, Doyle bought reams of paper and sheets of stamps. He wrote dozens and dozens of letters, and persuaded his friend to do the same. The hotel bellboy took great piles of these letters to be posted, thinking they were simply conducting business. The letter writing went on all night for two solid days. No sleep, just drinking, eating and writing, until Nathan Kingsley's fingers were crippled with writer's cramp. On the third day, something momentous took place.

Just after dawn, a flock of eighty chimney sweeps turned up at the house next door but one from where Henrietta Shelbourne was staying. The unfortunate widow who answered the door was speechless when she saw all the sweeps. They, in turn, were indignant, saying they had been summoned to her house by letter. Five coal wagons then turned up, followed by a fleet of furniture carts, a number of funeral hearses, and a string of hansom cabs carrying midwives, doctors, dentists and various guests. Then a convoy of beer wagons arrived from the Trueman Brewery in the East End, followed by a wagon carrying a pipe organ and seven carters pushing loads of potatoes. Three butchers then tried to squeeze into the packed street.

By noon, the Governor of the Bank of England had arrived, the Lord Chief Justice, the Lord Mayor of

London, and the Archbishop of Canterbury. The crowds went berserk when the Royal Coach appeared in the congested street, because the Duke of York, who was also Commander-in-Chief of the British Army, had been informed that his most decorated and loyal officer was dying at the widow's house. Then a Naval Chief turned up, and another wave of assorted people arrived to join the chaos. The congestion which followed was an early form of gridlock. The horses and carts were unable to move, and the area was soon redolent with the smell of innumerable steaming piles of horse manure. The brimming thoroughfare brought the centre of the capital to a halt.

In the middle of all this pandemonium, Daniel Doyle managed to forge his way through to Henrietta Shelbourne's house to claim his prize. The girl was looking out of her uncle's window, laughing at the riot of people and police jostling for space in the packed streets. She waved to Doyle, and he shouted up to her over the din: "I brought London to a standstill for you, now may I have your heart?"

Henrietta giggled childishly and placed her hand across her mouth. She shouted something to Doyle, who was standing pathetically amongst the heaving crowds on the pavement below. He had to strain his ears to catch what she was shouting over the incessant clamour. "I was pulling your leg!" she blithely cried, throwing her head back in delight.

A handsome young man suddenly appeared at the window and began kissing the girl's beautiful, slender neck. He too looked down at Doyle and guffawed when he saw his earnest face; disbelief and disappointment etched on its wrinkled features.

Daniel Doyle's heart was ripped apart. He returned to Liverpool with Nathan Kingsley a broken man, humiliated by his own folly. A well-known hoaxer named Theodore Hook was afterwards blamed for the so-called Berners Street Hoax, but although Hook revelled in the glory, he secretly admitted to friends that he was not behind the biggest practical joke that London has ever known. No one knew the true heartache that lay behind a jest perpetrated to win a lady's heart.

THE IMPRINT

Over the years, there have been several sightings of a certain ghost in the grounds of Wavertree's Blue Coat School after dark. A few years ago a policeman told me how a local resident reported seeing a grey-haired man roaming the playground at night, apparently searching for something, because he kept looking at the ground as he walked about. When the police arrived they found no one in the vicinity of the school.

The same figure was reported twice more that night, but whenever the police came, they could find no trace of any trespasser. For years it looked as if the identity of the Blue Coat School ghost would remain a mystery, until a listener to my radio show enlightened me. Arthur, a retired policeman, described the ghost in detail: the clothes it wore and exactly where it was seen. He then told me whose ghost it was, and the tale he related was very sad.

In the 1950s, Arthur's beat took in Smithdown Road and Church Road in Wavertree, right up past Picton Clock. One rainy night in November 1952, at around eleven o'clock, he was walking this beat, when he heard what sounded like a man crying, coming from inside the grounds of the Blue Coat School. He climbed over a wall and saw a man of about fifty with a mop of curly grey hair in a dark corner of the grounds. He was kneeling down, leaning on one hand.

Arthur slowly approached him and asked if he was alright, but he did not answer. In fact, he seemed to be unaware of the his presence. Deciding that the man was not really a threat, just a bit confused, or possibly drunk, he crouched down and said, "Cold tonight, isn't it?"

The man nodded with a look of infinite sadness, his eyes red and brimming with tears. Arthur looked down and saw that his hand was spread over the bottom one of the four steps leading to the playground. When he took his hand away, Arthur saw the imprint of a tiny hand in the step, obviously made by a child when the cement was wet. The man said his name was Tony and explained that the imprint was that of his daughter, Marjory. Five years ago, he had been taking his six-year-old daughter to school, when she had slipped from his grip. When he caught up with her she was in the playground of the Blue Coat School and had mischievously dipped her hand in the wet cement of the new steps. Marjorie thought it was really funny, and her father managed to get her out of the school playground before anyone noticed. Later that year, in December, she had been struck down with meningitis. She became critically ill and tragically died.

In the following year, Tony's wife divorced him and he turned to alcohol in an effort to try and cope with the loss of the little girl, who had been the apple of his eye. To make matters even worse, his wife had won custody of their son. Every now and then, Tony would stop off at the school on his way home from the pub to see and feel the imprint of his beloved Marjorie's hand on that step. He never got over the loss of his daughter and the collapse of his marriage, and was found dead near Wavertree Park from alcoholic poisoning.

Soon afterwards, the reports of his ghost being seen in the Blue Coat playground began. Today, the imprint of the girl's hand is barely visible, because the steps have been worn down by the feet of hundreds of children.

BLIGHTED LOVE

On Wavertree's Church Road, there is a church called the Holy Trinity, which dates from 1794. Facing it, on the other side of the road, are three ancient stone steps known locally as the mounting stone. From the late 1790s, churchgoers used to stand on these steps to mount their horses. Around 1800, a love affair began on those stone steps. Catherine Mayfield, the twenty-two-year-old daughter of local merchant, Alfred Mayfield, left Holy Trinity and returned to her horse, which was tethered to a post on Church Road. Her suitor, Joshua Quiller, a hard-headed businessman who owned paper factories in Liverpool and London, was neglecting her as usual, talking shop with several other businessmen who had just left the church service.

Catherine stood on the mounting stone, but the horse trotted off before she could mount and she clung awkwardly to its mane and saddle, with one foot caught in the stirrup. A youth of about eighteen seized the horse's reins and steadied her, bringing her back to the mounting steps, where Catherine was able to get into the saddle with some dignity. She thanked the lad, who had a mop of black curly hair and an attractive, open face, neither of which was lost on Catherine. He smiled at her and then walked away, but in those brief moments, something connected between them. It was love at first sight.

Catherine made secret enquiries about the youth, and

discovered that he was an orphan named Joel. He had been raised by a Jewish couple who gave him the name, but he ended up running away from home and had been living rough on the streets of Liverpool. He had been in trouble for hunting wood pigeons and other fowl on the various estates of Wavertree. In short, he was a vagabond. But 'when Jill's in love with Jack, his pockmarks seem like dimples', and so a well-to-do lady saw beyond the grimy image, and fell rapidly in love with the young vagrant.

Catherine persuaded her father, Alfred, to hire Joel to work on the sprawling acres of the family estate near what is now Menlove Avenue. That summer, she began a love affair with Joel that was somewhat absurd. The young man had a limited vocabulary and was almost slow-witted, and yet she ignored his shortcomings, noticing only his gentle side. He would collected posies of wild flowers for her, and on summer nights, the two of them would sit hidden under an old oak tree, gazing at the Milky Way and spotting shooting stars. Joel was in tune with nature, unlike Catherine's suitor, Joshua Quiller, who spoke about nothing but money.

In August, Catherine discovered that she was pregnant with Joel's child, and she visited an old friend of the family, Mrs Plaistow, for advice. Mrs Plaistow soon revealed her secret to a relative, and within a few days, the shocking news of the pregnancy reached the ears of Joshua Quiller. He was devastated and quickly turned to drink, but did not tell anyone about his sweetheart's infidelity and chose not to reveal to his beloved that he knew the awful truth. Instead, he bought an expensive wedding ring and visited Catherine late one night and asked for her hand in marriage. She gratefully accepted, deciding to pass off the child she was carrying as Joshua's. Catherine Quiller, as she now became, moved to London with her husband, who had purchased an enormous property on Hampstead Heath. In an apparent show of generosity, Joel was invited down to London to work on the estate by Joshua Quiller.

One day, Joel went missing without warning, leaving Catherine forlorn, as she still had strong feelings for him and was bearing his child. She asked her husband if he knew what had become of him, but he just shook his head. She suspected that he did know something, and more than likely had something to do with it.

On the following day, Catherine and Joshua were travelling across the old London Bridge in a carriage, when the vehicle was forced to a halt by huge crowds blocking the bridge. Joshua stepped out to see what was causing the disturbance. The crowds were looking over the bridge at something below. Curiosity got the better of Catherine, and she too left the carriage to see what was happening. One of the onlookers informed her that a pirate had been chained to the walls below London Bridge. The tide was coming in and soon he would be drowned. Catherine shuddered at the thought, although it was a common enough spectacle in those days.

She peeped over the bridge to see Joel shackled and chained to the bridge wall, the waves already lapping around his neck. Nauseous with shock, she almost passed out. Joshua slipped an arm around her and chuckled, gloatingly admitting that he had framed the youth and bribed the authorities to state that Joel had been found guilty of piracy. Catherine demanded to know why he had done such a cruel thing, and he jabbed at her stomach and vindictively hissed, "That child is not mine. It is his!"

Catherine turned away from him and pushed through the crowd, vaulting over the wall before anyone could stop her. A great commotion ensued as she dropped into the freezing waters of the Thames and witnesses said that she swam to

Joel and tried desperately to tear off the manacles, but the water rose relentlessly until it covered his head. She took great gulps of air and dived under the water to blow air it into her drowning lover's mouth, but it was useless. They both died, holding hands.

There is a gruesome footnote to this story. Joshua Quiller was buried in Highgate Cemetery, and in 1960, his grave had to be exhumed because of subsidence. His coffin had been split open by the roots of an ancient yew tree which had coiled itself around the corpse's neck. The end of the root appeared to come out of the mouth, as though Quiller's tongue had wrapped itself around his neck. The story later reached the ears of Emily Bronte, and she loosely based Heathcliff, a Liverpool waif, on the character of Joel.

THE KARMIC WHEEL

In Victorian times, Joseph Wigglesworth, a man who had lost both his legs in an accident at the age of thirteen, in 1830, used to sit for hours on a sort of cart on Pudsey Street. With no welfare state, Joe had to resort to playing a penny whistle to survive. His loyal mongrel dog Sandy was his only real friend, and used to perform tricks at a signal from Joe, but the financial return from these activities was paltry; nothing more than a few pennies and farthings in his cap. Joe was very independent though, and somehow scraped together enough money to cover the weekly rent for his tiny hovel in Bridport Street.

On a dismal February morning in 1860, a weeping rain fell from a low slate-grey sky. Joe was trying to inject a note of jollity into his playing, as he sat on the corner of Lime Street and Pudsey Street, when two finely dressed men in top hats stood before him. One of them began to talk about him in an offensive manner, looking in disdain at the single penny in his cap. They seemed to be fascinated by Sandy, who stood on her hind legs and raised her front paws in a begging gesture, with a comical hat strapped to her head. Edward Sims, a wealthy cotton broker, asked Joseph if his dog was for sale and produced a guinea, which he flipped about in his hand, trying to tempt him. Joe was starving, but he loved Sandy. He had raised her from an abandoned pup and she was all he had. "Sorry, sir, she isn't for sale."

Sims was furious and his colleague, Ferguson Bright, laughed and held out his hand. Edward Sims shuffled away swearing at the street beggar. With a grin, Mr Bright explained, "My friend claimed he could buy that old dog of yours, but he lost the wager."

On the following day, Joe was once again on the street, when top-hatted Edward Sims turned up with a policeman. "That is the accursed animal that attacked me, constable," he lied, pointing at Sandy with his cane. "It snapped at my heel on this beggar's orders, simply because I refused to give him money."

However, the policeman knew old Joseph Wigglesworth well. "I doubt that, sir," he replied. "That dog is no danger to the public. I pass here regularly on my beat, and the animal is a most peaceable creature."

Edward Sims flew into a rage and said that if the dog was not destroyed, he would report the constable to his superiors. Backed into a corner, the policeman had no choice but to concur, so he stroked Sandy and picked her up, crying out pitifully, "She's all I have in the world, please don't take her."

The policeman walked off to the police station holding

Sandy, who was still wearing her little hat. The dog yelped and looked back at its master, who seemed to have shrunk to almost nothing in his grief. Edward Sims accompanied the policeman to the station to make sure that the necessary form was filled in for the dog's destruction.

Joseph Wigglesworth was unable to raise a tune from his old penny whistle, and he curled up with his head bowed, as scalding tears formed rivulets down his grimy face.

People passing by who had not seen what had happened, thought it was just a cheap gimmick and passed by. As darkness fell, Joseph sadly made his way back to his dreary room; friendless in a cruel world. At one o'clock in the morning, he heard a scratching sound at the door. Using his hands, he pulled himself to the door and reached up to the handle. As soon as he had released it, the door flew open and in dashed Sandy. She licked Joe's face and danced around him yapping with excitement, having somehow escaped from the police station yard.

On the following morning, Joe set himself up near London Road, instead of his usual patch, because he was terrified of another encounter with Edward Sims. But later that day, Sims turned up once again and menacingly pointed his cane at the dog, threatening to have it destroyed. However, on this occasion, Sim's colleague Ferguson Bright, turned up and intervened. He argued that Sims was just a bad sport, who was being mean-spirited because he had lost a wager. An altercation ensued and Mr Bright said that if he bothered Joe again, he would impart certain information regarding his financial dealings to the authorities. That did the trick; Sims never troubled Joe again.

A year later, Edward Sims himself ended up as a cripple, when he was run down by a carriage in Edinburgh and his left leg had to be amputated below the knee. Not long afterwards, the Karmic wheel of Fate turned yet again, and Sims lost a fortune in a disastrous business venture.

Sandy died peacefully in her sleep five years later, and Joseph Wigglesworth played his penny whistle on the streets of Liverpool until he died of bronchitis in 1911, aged ninety-four.

THE KENSINGTON BANSHEE

In the 1950s, especially during the summer evenings, it was not unusual to see neighbouring families sitting on their doorsteps, or bringing out chairs to gossip over cups of tea and cigarettes. Their children usually played around them, so they could chatter away until long after midnight, especially at weekends and during the school holidays. This was the scene in 1959, at a certain street in the Kensington district of Liverpool. Two families, the McCabes and the Joneses, lived next door to one another, and one close July evening at nine o'clock, Mrs Jones came out of her house, curlers in, and plonked herself down on her chair. Her daughters followed with a bowl of warm water in which to soak her aching feet, and a little fold-up table upon which they laid a teapot, a jug of milk, cups, a bowl of sugar and so on. Then Mrs Jones's mother came out with a deckchair and pillow, and positioned herself by the bay window. Minutes later, Mr McCabe emerged in his string vest carrying two chairs, followed by his wife. She had sandwiches, a jar of pickled onions and a large bowl of blackcurrant jelly. Her little son sat on her knee, and her two daughters, Nora and Joan, perched on the ledge of the bay window in their nightdresses and slippers. Then someone let Terry, the little Jack Russell out. He ambled about the street, watching a few of the audacious cats slouching about.

The timing and atmosphere were perfect for a good all-nighter sort of 'jangle', and the Joneses and the McCabes set about discussing everyone's business in the street. They spent a good forty minutes talking about the comings and goings of the family who had just moved into Number 12; the Ryans, a large Irish family, complaining that they were always arguing and drunk, and seemed to have half of Ireland in their house. And they whispered that the young girl was not married to the man who had made her pregnant.

Anyway, this gossip was still going on at almost one o'clock in the morning, when suddenly, the two families heard someone crying. Terry the dog came hurtling down the road and bolted straight into the house. He was so terrified, he ran straight into the vestibule door and yelped with pain. Then Joan McCabe tapped her mother on the shoulder and gestured down the road, "Hey, Mam! Look at this!"

"Who is it?" she asked.

"Say nothing, Mam," said Mrs Jones, folding her arms over her ample bosom in disapproval.

A woman was staggering drunkenly down the street, stopping every now and then. She was dressed completely in black and her long hair covered her face. She stopped right in front of the Joneses and McCabes, and Mrs McCabe finally asked, "Are you alright, love?"

The figure said nothing, but moved on down the street towards Number 12, where the Ryans lived. Fourteen-year-old Nora set off after the weird looking woman, but was shocked to see that she had vanished. A moment later, an elderly man came down the street. It was Mr Ryan. When he saw them all sitting on their doorsteps, he stopped and surveyed the scene. "Who's having a jamboree at this hour?" he smiled jovially, hands on hips, obviously approving of the mini street party.

"Hey, one of your lot just passed us, Mr Ryan. She was in tears," said Mrs McCabe.

"Couldn't have been one of ours," said Mr Ryan, puzzled, "they're all in bed. They have to work in the morning, you see."

"Well, she went towards your house," said Mrs Jones.

"Wouldn't be my sister, May? Small woman with brown hair?"

"No, this one was old ... all in black. Her hair was grey, almost white ... and hanging down in front of her face."

Mr Ryan's friendly smile froze and he quickly made the sign of the cross. "Sweet Jesus," he said, almost inaudibly. "You just saw a banshee."

"A banshee?" laughed Mrs Jones uneasily.

"As true as you're all sitting there, it's a banshee. There'll be a death tonight." As he walked away, fumbling for his door key, they heard him muttering, "God Almighty".

Nora ran after him and tapped him on the shoulder, making him jump with fright. "Mr Ryan, will someone really die tonight?" she asked.

Mr Ryan nodded gravely, "Now, how can I explain it, child? The person who didn't hear or see the banshee in those two families will pass away."

Nora dashed back to report what he had said to the two families.

"He's drunk," said Mr McCabe dismissively. "Don't listen to him, he's only trying to frighten you." But deep down he felt very uneasy, because he had been the only one who had not seen the banshee.

On the following morning, Mr McCabe was found dead in his bed.

LAST WARLOCK IN WALES

At the outset of World War Two, in 1939, one million children were evacuated from the cities and towns of Britain. In Liverpool, thirteen-year-old Peter Raleigh and his eleven-year-old sister Maureen, of Sackville Street, in Everton, were sent to the relative safety of Gresford in Wales. Peter and Maureen, now in their seventies, told me that although these events took place over sixty-two years ago, to them it seems like only yesterday.

They were billeted to the home of a rather strange Welsh family, Mr and Mrs Shuker and their twenty-five-year-old daughter Olwyn. They were like people from a bygone age; all three dressed quaintly in dark Victorian-looking clothes. The living room of their granite cottage was dimly lit, the only modern item in the place, a crackly old radio. Mr Shuker looked about sixty-five and had a shock of white hair. His wife was small and round with rosy cheeks and had a perpetual grin on her face. Olwyn was very docile and never uttered a word, except to the bi black overweight cat, Chester. This cat did not take to the Raleigh children, and kept hissing at them and arching its back.

They were shown to their bedroom, which was little more than a tiny attic with a steeply sloping roof and a window under the eaves. Maureen opened the window and her eyes lit up, for directly outside, was an old apple tree with a branch bearing big red apples within easy reach. They leaned out and grabbed a few; fruit was a rare luxury in those times.

Mr Shuker took the children to the village sweetshop on the day of their arrival, and he struck them as being rather childish. Peter thought he was funny but Maureen considered him just plain silly. As they were returning from the shop, he said, "Watch this children," and pointed to the village constable who was walking along ahead of them. He adjusted his gait so that he was walking in step with him. Peter giggled and fell into step behind him, but Maureen was embarrassed and looked about to see if anyone was watching. Mr Shuker walked in perfect synchronisation with the bobby, then all of a sudden, pretended to trip, and at that exact moment, the policeman fell over.

"How did you do that?" asked Peter.

Mr Shuker grinned like a mischievous child and said, "Resonance!" Without further explanation, he walked on and helped up the baffled policeman.

Another time, in the following year, Mrs Shuker suddenly went to the window and looked up at the night sky, saying that German planes were on the way. About twenty minutes later, the unmistakable low droning sound of enemy bombers could be heard over the cottage, on their way to bomb Liverpool. Maureen thought her foresight creepy.

Once, Maureen passed Olwyn Shuker's bedroom and, seeing the door open, peeped in. She was holding two weird-looking dolls and muttering something in Welsh. Maureen watched, fascinated, as she cut off a long lock of her hair, then used it to bind the two effigies together. Her cat suddenly mewed shrilly, and Olwyn caught the Liverpool girl looking in at her and told Maureen that it was rude to spy on people. All the same, she invited her in and showed her the creepy effigies, which were made from clay, saying they represented herself and a man in the village. The effigies bound with hair were part of an elaborate love spell to make the man fall for her. Maureen was amazed when, a short time later, she saw plain-faced Olwyn linking arms with a handsome young man in the village.

The most startling revelation came one Sunday when Maureen finally asked Mr Shuker to his face if he was a sort of witch. His answer astounded her. "I am a warlock, the last warlock in Wales." Maureen and Peter were enthralled as he showed them his wardrobe. Among the old garments, was a long black silken gown, adorned with strange symbols, stars, crescents and so on. It was obviously a magician's robe. There was also a pointed black cap and in a corner of the wardrobe, what looked like a quiver of arrows. Mr Shuker explained that these were consecrated wands made of rowan – magic wands!

Something caught Peter's eye and he asked what the large yellow chunk of glass was that he could see in the wardrobe. Mr Shuker picked it up and told them it was polished amber and took it downstairs where he rubbed it with a black cloth, set it in front of the table and drew the curtains. A candle was lit, and Mr Shuker put his elbows on the table and stared intently at the amber. He suddenly began to shake, his face contorted, and tears rolled down his face. He threw a black cloth over the amber, then turned to look at the children, as if about to break bad news to them, but he said nothing.

When the time came for the evacuees to go home, having said goodbye to Mrs Shuker and Olwyn, Mr Shuker walked them to Wrexham train station. It started to rain heavily so Peter put on his school cap, but Maureen began to fret when she realised she had forgotten her umbrella. "Don't worry, you won't get wet," said Mr Shuker, and they didn't; the rain seemed to fall all around them, but not on them. He gave the children one last hug, unabashed tears streaming down his cheeks, as he waved to them from the platform.

Back home, they were devastated to learn that their Auntie Joan had been killed during the Blitz – on the same night that Mr Shuker had cried after gazing into the piece of amber. Could he have seen Joan's death in the amber? Was this why he had been so upset? To add to the mystery, when Maureen went up to her bedroom, she found the umbrella she had left in the Shuker's cottage lying on her bed.

MILLIONAIRE TRAMP

In 1965 twenty-year-old Jimmy Hughes left his Scotland Road home to get away from his drunken father. His mother had died a few years before, leaving him heartbroken because she had always encouraged and spoiled him, despite being poor, to compensate for his drunken father. So his childhood had been full of love. Jimmy moved into a bedsit in the Dingle and found himself a job in the YMCA on Mount Pleasant, working in the kitchen, mopping floors, making beds and cleaning tables in the dining area. He was a really hard worker.

One evening he went to a place called the Sink Club, on Hardman Street, because it only cost two-and-six to get in and it was there that he met a pretty blonde-haired girl from Thingwall, on the Wirral. Her name was Penny Johnson, and from the way she spoke and her manners, Jimmy could tell that she was middle-class. Even so, he and Penny really hit it off, and ended up leaving the club together. They hailed a taxi which took them to a house on Ullet Road, where Penny was staying for a few days with her cousin. Unknown to her, Jimmy was so skint, that he walked home in the pouring rain to his dingy bedsit in the Dingle, but he did not care because he was in love. The only problem was that he had told Penny that he owned his own garage on Roscoe Street, to impress her. He was too proud to admit to working in the 'YM' as they used to call it.

On top of all that, Penny had suggested going on a date to a restaurant during the following week, when she would be staying at her cousin's again. Jimmy had suggested Reece's Grill Room in Clayton Square. He wanted to give her a great night out, so he asked a few people for a loan, but no one would lend him anything.

On the following day, disaster struck. Jimmy was cleaning the YMCA kitchen when he saw an amusing sight. Several rows of cakes, pies and sausage rolls had been laid out on a table, ready to be put into a display cabinet, when, suddenly, a hand emerged from under the tablecloth, groped around for a cake, then grabbed it. Jimmy drew a few people's attention to the spectacle, but the manager did not see the funny side and lifted the tablecloth to reveal an old man in a dirty dufflecoat, squatting underneath with crumbs all over his beard. The manager recognised him as a tramp who had been seen around the place recently and whose name was believed to be Cassidy. Some people called him Grandad. That was all that was known about him.

The manager told him to leave, but he refused, so the police were called. In a whisper, Jimmy Hughes advised him to disappear before they arrived, but the tramp smiled at him. There was something in his eyes which set him apart from the usual meth-soaked tramps seen in the streets. Something melancholic and intelligent flickered in his China blue eyes. There was a lot of hurt in those eyes, but who had inflicted the pain, and what sad history lay within remained a mystery.

When the manager saw Jimmy Hughes letting the tramp escape via the staff door he was furious, "That's it, Mr Hughes, you're sacked! Instant dismissal," he barked.

Jimmy was devastated. It was Thursday, pay day, and he would not be getting his wages now. How on earth could he take Penny out? He felt sick at heart. It was at this point that something unbelievable happened. As Jimmy Hughes was dejectedly donning his coat, the tramp came back in through the staff door. In a well-spoken voice, reminiscent of James Mason, he said, "I'm sorry they gave you the sack, because you helped me."

"Oh, that's okay," said Jimmy, trying to raise a smile, whilst feeling sick inside.

The tramp reached into his pocket and took out an old leather wallet. His grimy fingers flipped through a wad of crisp banknotes which he offered to Jimmy, who was struck dumb when he realised what they were. The notes were of denominations he had never even seen before, in shades of purple and red. They were one hundred pound notes. The tramp had just given him about ten of these notes, and he still had a wad of them left in his wallet.

"You're a good man," said Cassidy, who then promptly left before Jimmy could ask any questions.

Jimmy Hughes chased after him, shouting down the street, but he had melted into the crowds. He later heard that the tramp was supposed to have been a millionaire who chose to live as a hobo. A newsagent in Mount Pleasant said he had been a tycoon who had suffered a breakdown over a failed romance, and he had chosen to live on the streets in an attempt to forget her. He was a common figure in the hostel in Shaw Street.

By the way, Jimmy and Penny did have their date that night. They later married, and now live on the Isle of Man.

THE MAN WHO
REPORTED HIS OWN MURDER

One wintry night in the north of Liverpool, in 1932, a bowler-hatted man walked into Rose Hill Police Station. The desk sergeant, a Mr Davies, was enjoying a cup of tea at the time. The man, who was about forty-five, walked up to the counter and coolly stated, "I'd like to report a murder, sergeant." Sergeant Davies gulped down his tea and grabbed the log book. "A murder?" he repeated, pencil at the ready.

"Yes, that's right," said the man in a matter-of-fact tone.

"Do you happen to know the victim, sir?" he asked, without looking up.

"Yes, it's me!" came the reply.

The sergeant closed the log book and sighed. The station had more than its fair share of unbalanced characters making ludicrous statements. "Really sir? Well you're looking quite well, considering. Is there a full moon out there tonight?"

"Sergeant, I have just been killed, I am quite serious," answered the man sternly.

"Go on then," smirked the sergeant, who had resumed drinking his tea. "Who killed you?"

"A mechanic called Frank Draper ... from Boundary Street. I paid him to fix my brakes but he botched the job. I've just crashed into a wall on Vauxhall Road. I'm dead because of him."

Sergeant Davies scrutinised the man more carefully; there was something spooky about him and he left the counter to enlist the help of a young constable to escort the unstable individual out of the station. However, when they came back, there was no sign of him.

About forty minutes later, Sergeant Davies was told by a policeman from the dock road beat that a car had crashed into a wall on Vauxhall Road. It appeared that the driver, who was from Scotland Road, had probably died instantly. Apparently he had been wearing a bowler hat, just like the sinister man who had visited the police station. Out of curiosity, Sergeant Davies visited Boundary Street, and came across a sign over a garage that read 'Frank Draper, Car Mechanic'. Davies called into the garage and discovered that Mr Draper had indeed been paid to fix the brakes of the vehicle that had crashed on Vauxhall Road.

A policeman convinced Sergeant Davies, against his better judgement, to visit the morgue to view the crash victim. When the body was wheeled out, Davies recoiled in horror. There could be no mistake, it was, without doubt, the man who had come into the station to report his own death.

An inquiry into the fatal crash established that it had been caused by the vehicle's badly adjusted brakes …

THE PENDLE NECROMANCER

When a man of the cloth tells you a strange story, it does make it sound more convincing. The following story was told to me early in 2001, by a vicar who has now retired in Liverpool. I have obviously had to change a few details to preserve his anonymity.

In the long hot summer of 1976, thirty-five-year-old Jeff, from Liverpool, finally ended his four years as a curate when he was ordained and given his own church. Some of the parishioners, and one young lady in particular, soon caught his attention. Her name was Samantha; a beautiful woman of about twenty with long black hair and a rather anaemic looking face. What really attracted him to her was her eyes, which were hypnotic and very seductive.

Delivering his sermon in the pulpit on his first Sunday in the new parish, the new vicar started to stammer and lose his thread. The older members of the congregation tutted, because they realised that he was continually glancing at Samantha, who was sitting on the front pew, dressed provocatively in a very short skirt. Two elderly ladies started to give little coughs of disapproval, but Jeff manfully continued with his sermon, which was about upholding the Commandments. For some reason, he suddenly could not remember them all, despite being very familiar with them. He apologised profusely, saying it was his first sermon, as he shuffled through his notes and struggled to continue.

Then the two ladies who had coughed deliberately moments earlier suddenly started to cough again – only this time they both seemed to be having an asthma attack. They rose to their feet in distress going red in the face. Two men ushered them out into the fresh air and they soon recovered.

That night, the vicar had the most realistic dream he had ever had, in which he was making passionate love to Samantha. As he woke up, he felt as if her lips were still pressing against his mouth. He became madly infatuated with the girl, but she seemed to have little interest in him.

Two months later, Samantha's aunt, an Irish woman, passed away, and Samantha had the body put in an open coffin so that her relatives could pay their respects. The vicar bought a floral tribute and decided that he would visit her and say that, although he had not known her aunt, he was sure she was a lovely woman – a transparent ploy to get acquainted with the delectable Samantha.

So Jeff went over to Samantha's home at about 7.30pm, clutching his ostentatious bouquet. As he walked up the dark path to the house, he got the shock of his life. By the faint light of the coal fire inside, he could see Samantha – and she was completely naked. Jeff was a man of the cloth, but he was also a flesh and blood man, and he could not resist such temptation. He walked up to the ground floor window with his heart pounding in his ears and peeped through the window. Through a gap in the curtains he could clearly see her prancing around in front of the fire like a woman possessed. Behind her, on a stand, was the open coffin containing her late aunt, who had her arms crossed over her chest.

Jeff tried to move away from the window, yet he just could not keep his eyes off the naked young woman. In his mind he apologised to God, then cautiously peeped back through the window to find that another naked girl had joined Samantha. She was dancing about as well and Jeff thought he could hear someone singing in the house. Then he saw something that sent him hurtling away from the house. The body in the coffin started moving; the arms slowly uncrossing as the girls continued their manic dance. The vicar dropped the expensive flowers and sped off into the night, all amorous thoughts banished from his mind.

The funeral took place later that week, but as Jeff was conducting the service, he wondered if Samantha's aunt was actually in the coffin, as he now realised that she and the other woman must be part of a witches' coven. He told his superiors about his experiences, but they were not interested. Some time later, he met and married another local woman, but for years he was reminded of the experience when sinister effigies were left on his doorstep. He also received many poison pen letters until he finally moved to another parish, far away from the area.

PEEPING TOM

The following events took place in the late nineteenth century in an area of Birkenhead bounded by Watson Street, Duke Street, Cleveland Street and North Conway Street.

One windy January night, in 1885, Rosanna Cuff, a young serving girl, was peeling potatoes in the scullery of a Brook Street house, when she felt a tingling sensation on the nape of her neck; a sensation of being watched. She spun round and looked through the top pane of the long kitchen windows, where a full moon was just visible between the curtains. Her gaze then turned to the lower panes, and there, between a small gap, she saw what she later described as a pair of evil, yet smiling eyes. Rosanna let out a yelp, and fled headlong out of the kitchen to tell her master, Edward Manney Jones, who was almost eighty. Despite his age, Manney Jones, accompanied by his butler, ran into the backyard, the latter brandishing a poker, and Mr Manney Jones an old sword, but the prowler was nowhere to be seen. This was just the start, and more and more reports of the peeping Tom flooded into the local police station.

A housewife on Watson Street had been soaking in a tin bath at midnight in front of the dying embers of her kitchen fire, when she too spotted a face at her window. The lower half was hidden behind a dark scarf, the head covered in a cap of some sort. The naked woman covered her breasts and threw a bar of soap at the window before screaming for her husband. The voyeur was also seen gazing lustfully through the basement window of a house on Price Street at two young maids who were playfully dancing with each other.

The police stepped up their patrols, but the peeking pervert's escapades became ever more audacious. At a lodging house near Duke Street, a buxom young lady awoke to find a letter on her bedside cabinet, which read: 'I could have had you last night. I left my mark on your face.' She rushed to a mirror and was horrified to find two black smears on each cheek. They seemed to have been made by soot being wiped on to her face by someone's finger.

News of the daring intruder spread like wildfire, and within a fortnight, there were five reports of girls and women waking up to find soot-marks on their faces and breasts. One widow screamed out in the dead of night bringing every member of her family rushing into her bedroom, but it had been a false alarm; the family cat had merely brushed its tail against her face as she slept. In the meantime, the hunt went on for the peeping Tom and speculation was rife as to his true identity.

A local fishmonger, Peter Jones, became a suspect after a woman claimed that she had often caught him squinting through keyholes when he was younger. A butcher on Watson Street conjectured that the peeping Tom was a certain elderly policeman who had become sex-crazed after his wife had deserted him, and a well-to-do businessman, Harold Gaines, of Park Road, offered a reward of five hundred pounds for information that would lead to the apprehension of the nocturnal snooper. Gaines was flabbergasted when he awoke one morning to be told that his maid-of-all-work and cook, both women in their thirties, had both found soot marks on their faces and undergarments. This time he had been clever enough to get past front and back doors, bolted top and bottom.

One stormy night a few weeks later, a habitual drunk, Alfie Randles, had just walked home to his house on Park Road and was trying to fit his key into the lock, but kept missing the keyhole. Frustrated, he tried the doorknob, and to his surprise, the door opened. He staggered inside and noticed that a new gas mantle had been installed, and flocked wallpaper now hung in the lobby. He wondered where his wife had got the money from, so he went into the sitting room to ask her, but she was not there. The parlour looked entirely different to the drunken Randles, until he slowly realised that he had walked into the wrong house. Not only that, he had also unwittingly stumbled upon the house of the mysterious peeping Tom.

A man stood there in black clothing, the lower half of his face hidden behind a black silk scarf, whilst on his head he wore a river pilot's black leather cap, with the peak pulled down over his eyes. He reached for a poker and charged at Alfie Randles, whose legs were wobbly with terror. He ran into the hallway, almost wrenched the knob off the vestibule door, then threw himself at the front door. Once out of the house, he stumbled down the steps, whimpering.

The door behind him slammed shut, and the number upon that door – fifty-four – was the number of Harold Gaines's house. He must be the peeping Tom! The police were alerted and several officers pounded on the door. The neighbours crowded round and when Mr Gaines finally opened the door in his nightshirt, the police stormed the house. A full hour passed before they re-emerged, and when they did so, Mr Gaines stood smiling in his doorway, bidding them goodnight. Rumours abounded that he had bribed the policemen.

The peeping Tom reports ceased from that night on, but just under a year later, Harold Gaines died from pneumonia. Days after his death, people reported seeing a pair of eyes gazing at them through their windows – including one second floor window! Most people believed the peeping Tom was the ghost of Harold Gaines, still snooping from beyond the grave!

GHOSTLY PIANO

In 1966, twenty-two-year-old Nancy moved into a terraced house in a certain street off Upton Park Road, not far from Birkenhead Park. Nancy was a very innocent girl, though quite sociable, and it was not long before she met a young man in the area. His name was Bobby and he worked in a local factory. His weekly wage was pretty meagre, but he was a very proud and honest person who refused to take money off anyone, especially Nancy. When Nancy's beloved grandmother had died, she had left Nancy a small fortune, so she did not need to work for a while. Bobby felt somewhat intimidated by the situation, because he felt he should be the breadwinner.

Before Nancy met Bobby, she had made friends with Audrey, a thirty-year-old woman from a large family off Upton Park Road; she and Nancy got on really well. They had even been to a few clubs together, and Nancy had stayed over with Audrey's family a few times.

One Saturday night, Nancy and Bobby went to the Cavern Club in Liverpool, and while they were dancing, Nancy noticed that he was not his normal cheerful self and seemed to have something playing on his mind. She took him aside and asked him what was wrong, but was unable to hear his reply because of the thumping of the live band. Frustrated and annoyed because he was spoiling their evening, she ended up storming out on him.

He caught up with her at the Pier Head, where they ended up drinking coffee and discussing their future. Bobby said he had heard a strong rumour that the factory he had been working in might be closing in the near future, and he would have to find a better job. Until then, he would somehow have to find enough money to be able to take her out and buy her things. Nancy told him not to be so stupid, because she loved him anyway.

Nancy got back that night to find that her house had been burgled. Money she kept in a drawer had been taken, along with her television, radio and a few other items. Then she ran into the back parlour. Her most prized possession had gone: an antique Collard & Collard upright piano. It had belonged to her grandmother and was worth hundreds of pounds. From the scrape-marks on the floor, they could easily see that the thieves had taken it out of the back door. The alleyway was a short distance from a road where a van had probably been waiting to spirit it away. There had been no forced entry, so a key must have been used. The police investigated and just said they would keep a look out for the piano in antique shops and secondhand stores.

On the following day, Bobby did not turn up at Nancy's and she sat in the parlour with her best friend Audrey in a depressed state. Then she received another shock. Audrey said, "Just between you and me, Nancy, I think Bobby had something to do with the break-in." Nancy was furious at the suggestion, saying it was a ridiculous idea; Bobby loved her. Audrey pointed out that she knew hardly anything about him and then she dropped a bombshell. "Nancy, please don't repeat this, but did you know that Bobby knocks around with robbers?"

"My Bobby? Where did you hear such a thing?"

Audrey had seen him drinking with well-known house-breakers. "I don't want to hurt you, but I think he probably gave your spare key to a friend and they had a copy made."

"No, not my Bobby. He loves me," Nancy insisted.

"Nancy, where is he tonight then? They say a guilty

conscience needs no accuser. I bet he won't come near you again," predicted Audrey, bluntly.

Nancy burst into tears. It all made sense now. That was why he had been preoccupied in the Cavern; he knew his friends were breaking into her house and must have felt guilty about it. Audrey comforted her and took her round to her own house, where the family tried to cheer her up. They sat her at the head of the table and Audrey's mother served her a fine meal.

At eleven o'clock that night, Nancy and all Audrey's family heard the sounds of a piano; a piano playing a familiar melody, 'No Place Like Home'. Nancy stood up and said, "That's my piano! That's the song my grandmother always played." Audrey's family looked at each other, mystified. Then, turning to Audrey, she asked, "Audrey, is my piano in this house? It is, isn't it?"

Audrey assured her that it certainly was not, and seemed hurt and stung by the accusation.

"Well where's that noise coming from then?" Nancy asked, exasperated, and marched out into the hallway.

From there it was obvious that the music was coming from next door, where a respectable elderly couple lived. She hammered on the door and an old man answered, with his elderly wife hovering behind him, looking bewildered. She barged past them, followed by Audrey and two of her brothers. There, in the parlour, they found the antique piano, playing 'No Place Like Home' all by itself. As everyone looked on, the ghostly keys stopped playing.

The police later discovered that the old man's son, also the local window cleaner, had seen the piano in Nancy's back parlour during his rounds, and had got a local crook to pick the back door lock. The window cleaner had then stored the stolen piano at his parents' home. Nancy also discovered that Audrey had been making approaches to Bobby behind her back and had tried to make Nancy finish with him by insinuating that he associated with crooks. Nancy asked Bobby if her approaches had been the thing that had been bothering him and he admitted that it was, but then reassured her that she was the only girl for him.

The couple subsequently married and to this day, Nancy believes that it was the ghost of her beloved grandma who played the piano that night.

GLADSTONE'S ATLANTIS BILL

At Number 62 Rodney Street, there is a plaque which reads: 'Gladstone, four times Prime Minister, born in this house, 29th December 1809'. Gladstone was an impressive reformer, legislator and legendary orator who dominated politics alongside his Conservative opponent, Disraeli. Gladstone was not an imaginative man, but a tough politician, who produced the Home Rule Bills and strove in the midst of controversy to bring peace to Ireland's troubles. Imagine then, how astonished the members of the House of Commons were, in 1886, when Prime Minister Gladstone rose to his feet and attempted to get a bill through Parliament. Not a reform bill, but 'a bill to furnish funds to search for the legendary sunken continent of Atlantis'.

His bill was met with hoots and howls of derisive laughter from the benches on both sides of the House; many thinking the seventy-seven-year-old Prime Minister had suddenly become senile, and Gladstone's astonishing proposal was defeated. Many also wondered what had convinced the steady and practical Gladstone to seek funds for such an outlandish expedition.

There were two reasons: in secret, Gladstone had read a book about Atlantis, an island said to have vanished below the Atlantic in the middle of the night, some 10,500 BC. The book, by American Congressman Ignatius Donnelly, had captured his imagination; he had also recently heard about an incredible incident concerning Lancashire adventurer, James T Morgan. About two years previously, Morgan had been returning to Liverpool from Brazil, where he had been exploring the Matto Grosso and the Amazon for gold. When the ship was in the middle of the Atlantic, about nine hundred miles from the Azores, a lookout spotted a dark, triangular mass a few miles distant.

By early evening, the ship was within a mile of the mass and the captain and crew could see the tip of an enormous black pyramid projecting out of the water. The ship's compass started spinning wildly, as if the pyramid was magnetic. The Brazilian captain fully intended to sail straight on by, but Morgan urged him not to. The captain grudgingly relented and allowed Morgan and four of the crew to row a lifeboat over to the pyramid to take a brief look. The structure was made of basalt, and was estimated to have been twice as high as the Great Pyramid at Giza, in Egypt; a staggering 960 feet in height. Ledge-like steps went halfway up the structure, and Morgan attempted to climb them, but they were coated with slippery marine vegetation, which rendered them far too treacherous for him to proceed any further.

Morgan and the crewmen returned to the ship and made further measurements of the pyramid using the ship's instruments. It obviously continued downwards underwater for quite a distance, so estimating its true dimensions was impossible. During the night, a strange faint glow, like St Elmo's fire, gathered around its tip, but at three o'clock in the morning, the captain insisted they set sail for Liverpool, in order to keep his deadline.

When other ships surveyed the same area, some months later, there was no sign of the mysterious dark pyramid. It was as if it had plunged back into the depths of the Atlantic from whence it came. Could the pyramid have been the remains of an Atlantean temple, thrust to the surface by some volcanic upheaval, only to sink back into oblivion?

ROMAINE OF RODNEY STREET

In the 1920s and 1930s, a strange character named Alaric Romaine lived at Number 16 Rodney Street. At that time, in the front page columns of the *Liverpool Echo*, Romaine was advertised as, 'a private detective who gets results'. Romaine remains something of a mystery. He was described as being of foreign appearance; some said he was Hungarian. What was unusual about him was his unorthodox detection methods, in that he claimed to occasionally be able to read minds. He also claimed an ability to receive psychic impressions from objects found at the scene of a crime, which enabled him to piece together what had happened.

In January 1930, Clara Simmons called on Mr Romaine at his Rodney Street office, bringing with her a small photograph of a handsome looking man with a pencil moustache, whom she said was her brother Robert. She recounted how she had had a petty argument with him some months ago and he had not been in touch since. When she asked Romaine if he could use his unique powers to find him, he did a curious thing; he asked her if he could study her palm. Clara duly offered him her hand. With his index finger, Romaine gently traced the fine lines on her palm and Clara seemed fascinated. However, this was actually a gimmick for reading a person's mind; a technique learned from the Indian fortune tellers during his days in Delhi, in which they distract a person by getting them to focus their attention on their hand. When a person drops his guard in this way, it is supposedly possible to read their mind. Romaine suddenly let go of the woman's palm.

"Robert isn't your brother ... he's your lover!" he declared dramatically, "and you are a married woman." Clara Simmons gasped but Romaine persisted. "You are carrying his baby and he has deserted you. You want me to find him, of course."

Miss Simmons ended her charade and gave a little sob. Romaine felt pity for her and said, "The father of your child lives on the south coast now. I see water. I'd say Bournemouth or Brighton."

Clara then confided that Robert's family was from Boscombe, a suburb of Bournemouth. Whether she ever caught up with her errant lover is not known.

On another occasion, a Mr Ling, from Chinatown, visited Romaine to report that someone had been stealing from his home. He could not go to the police because he kept large amounts of opium on his premises, and they had also been stolen. Romaine visited the scene of the crime and picked up a sort of psychic trail, like a bloodhound following its nose, which led to Mr Ling's brother-in-law. Mr Ling was furious, and called Romaine a charlatan, but Romaine told him to check the cellar of his brother-in-law's house. Sure enough, in the cellar's floor safe, Mr Ling found the stolen opium and other expensive items taken from his home.

In 1939, upon the outbreak of war, Romaine was summoned to Whitehall to help the fight against the Nazis in an operation code-named 'Green Mirror'. Romaine and a group of skilled magicians and illusionists, including a gifted music hall conjuror, Jasper Maskelyne, hid tanks, armies, and even an entire harbour. If you write to the Public Records Office and ask to see copies of the files on Romaine, or Maskelyne, the London bureaucrats will tell you that the files are not due to be released until 2021.

They somehow created images of British warships in the English Channel and made Montgomery's 150,000 troops, with 1,000 guns and tanks, invisible to Rommel. However, Romaine and Maskelyne's greatest achievement was making an entire harbour vanish. This was Alexandria harbour in Egypt. They had all the harbour lights turned off and then recreated the same pattern of lights in the desert. Around these lights, Romaine had explosive charges planted. When the German bombers flew over Alexandria, they saw the harbour was further to the west than they had expected and re-calibrated their instruments. As they started dropping bombs, Romaine set off the explosives around the lights, so it looked as if both cargo and ships were going up in flames. The real harbour, a few miles to the East, survived the night raid.

These were just some of the things Romaine of Rodney Street was involved in, but in 2021, the world will finally discover the full truth about him.

BRING BACK MY DANNY TO ME

A reformed drug addict told me this story, and his counsellor and several other people have backed it up. I have had to change a few names for obvious reasons.

In 1996, thirty-six-year-old Danny was at a nightclub in Birkenhead, when a friend pestered him to try cocaine. He resisted at first and his so-called friends accused him of being a bore, but in the end, he snorted the dangerous powder. Before long, his friends were persuading him to try ecstasy. At this point, Danny could not understand all the fuss about drugs, because he felt in control of them; just like having a cup of tea when you felt like one, he thought.

Then his life started to fall apart. His girlfriend left him for another man and the firm he worked for went into liquidation and Danny ended up on state benefits. His cocaine habit spiralled out of control and he began stealing to feed his addiction. Through constant use, the cocaine seemed to have lost its effect, so Danny decided to try heroin to recover the buzz, and descended into a personal hell. His life revolved around getting the next fix and he became anti-social and paranoid. His parents were dead, and the aunt he looked upon as his mother was gravely ill in hospital, so he had no one to turn to.

Sweating and shaking from cold turkey, Danny foolishly rushed round to his dealer with a knife demanding heroin, promising to pay him soon. The dealer's lackeys soon caught up with him and beat him to within an inch of his life. They bundled him into the boot of a car and dumped him in a derelict house in a run-down Birkenhead street in the dead of night. He was left frozen and trembling and barely able to move because of his injuries. Like a wounded

animal, he eventually crawled up into a ball in a corner of the filthy room whimpering helplessly.

Then Danny noticed something out of the corner of his eye. In the old fire grate, which was filled with rubble and all manner of filth, a golden light flickered. Then a wonderful aroma filled his nostrils – the smell of something cooking. The lopsided dust-covered lampshade began to glow, revealing the contents of the strangely familiar room; an old sofa, two armchairs, a dining table, overlaid with an immaculate cloth, on which was a quaint, tall, narrow-necked milk bottle, or 'sterry' bottle, as Danny recalled. Butter on a little dish, a plate of bread, a bowl of sugar and a bottle of 'Cheerio' sauce were also on the table. These simple items reminded him of another place where there had once been love. A broadsheet copy of the *Liverpool Echo* was draped over the arm of an armchair, together with a comic called *The Sparky*. The fire in the grate seemed to warm Danny's frozen soul.

What happened next made him really sit up and take notice, because in walked the woman he had idolised all his childhood, his grandmother. She had raised him after his parents had died within six months of one another. His heart sighed and in disbelief he whispered, "Gran!" unable to believe she was actually there, for surely she had died years ago? That terrible day when he had found her dead in her armchair, and he had cried his eyes out as he tried desperately to wake her up. His grandmother walked over to him carrying a bowl of steaming scouse. "Come on, lad, come and get your tea," she beamed.

"Okay, Gran," Danny said, struggling to his feet.

He sat in his old chair, the one his grandmother used to tell him he would break if he kept rocking it backwards, and devoured the delicious scouse, which seemed to nourish his

mind as well as his body. Then came the homemade apple pie and 'Bird's' custard. His grandmother suddenly leaned over the table, wet her fingers, and brushed his straggly fringe aside, like she had always done and then put his copy of the *Sparky* on the table. "Wasn't sure if you'd read that one," she smiled.

"No, I haven't, Gran, thanks." He got up, walked round the table and held out his arms to her. The only love that could never die, he thought, the love for your grandmother. She hugged him, and soon he was sobbing like a baby, "I've missed you, Gran. I've really missed you."

"Ahh, come on, sulks, don't cry," she cooed, then added, "I have to go soon, Danny."

"Oh no, Gran, please don't," he pleaded.

"I only came back to ask you a favour."

"What is it, Gran?" asked Danny, eager to do anything to keep her there. "You want me to go on an errand for you?"

"I want my little Danny back. Please be good for your Gran, son bun. Don't put needles in your arm, please."

As Danny promised to beat his addiction, the room darkened, taking the fire, the table and everything else with it. Then he felt those fingers again, affectionately brushing his fringe. He stumbled out of that derelict house and realised that it had once been his childhood home.

Danny was admitted to hospital, and subsequently made a miraculous recovery, thanks to a patient drugs counsellor. He is now drug free, has a steady job, and is renovating the house where his grandmother's ghost came back from the grave to save the child she loved.

SHIRO NINJA

Up until the 1970s, a mysterious three-storey house stood on the corner of Crown Street and Grinfield Street, in the Edge Hill district of Liverpool. The windows were always shuttered, even in summer, and the only person who really knew the occupants was the coalman. He knew both the elderly oriental-looking Mr Kan and his servant, Mr Tenshi.

One freezing January morning, in the late 1920s, the coalman was delivering fuel via an alleyway that ran from Smithdown Lane, when he witnessed a brutal incident. A young, timid looking man, of about sixteen or seventeen, was being beaten up by a gang of half a dozen ruffians. They had pushed him into the alleyway and robbed him of his shoes and the few pennies he had in his pockets. The teenager was left semi-conscious after the coalman intervened and the gang ran off. The criminals were members of the notorious Tierney gang, named after their leader, Jim Tierney. The gang also specialised in robbing railway goods off the trains in Crown Street.

Hearing the commotion, old Mr Kan came out of his backyard and helped the victim into his home. The coalman followed and watched as herbal medicine was administered to the youth, who gave his name as Patrick Munn. An orphan since he was twelve, he had been living hand-to-mouth ever since and was underweight and badly under-nourished.

Mr Kan took pity on him and resolved to take him under his wing. Every week or so the coalman would note how Patrick was changing for the better. His physique improved steadily, and one day, he was amused to see Mr Kan's servant shaving his head. The months went by and Kan taught him how to defend himself using martial arts. He drank only water, and ate only rice, oatmeal, raw meat, or uncooked fish. The transformation was unbelievable.

During one visit, the coalman watched Mr Kan showing Patrick how to punch through a hard wooden board. Kan said, "Don't punch the board; punch at a point just beyond it," and demonstrated by smashing his fist right through it. Another time, Kan tied a rope around Patrick's ankle, and threaded it over the wheel of a ceiling pulley in the washroom. When he pulled on the rope, Patrick's leg rose until it was vertical and eventually he could raise his leg vertically without the aid of the rope. Mr Kan would laugh and call the boy 'Shiro Ninja', which means 'white Ninja' in Japanese. He dropped the name Patrick and instead called him 'Mono', meaning one, which was to be his new name.

Mono became very adept in the ancient Japanese art of fighting. He was an excellent student, according to Mr Kan, and the coalman would often watch, spellbound, as he and Mono sparred in the large backyard. Despite his age, Kan's reflexes were like lightning. The two of them would also sit in the yard meditating for hours. The coalman was once told that it was possible for a Ninja to tell the time of day by looking into the eye of a cat. At noon, the cat's iris is a perfectly vertical slit, and there were then seven gradual changes that corresponded to the hours of the day as the sun moved across the sky.

One Sunday evening, in an alleyway off Mason Street, Mr Kan and his protege were on their way to visit a friend, when the Tierney gang surrounded them. One of them produced a cosh and tapped his hand with it menacingly, as he joked about Mr Kan's pigtail. Now, in the police files, there is a fascinating record of the injuries suffered by the infamous gang members after the confrontation which ensued. Of the seven present, five of them between them sustained a fractured jaw, a broken arm, multiple shin fractures, concussion, and one attacker had his spleen ruptured and came within a hair's breadth of death. One person alone was responsible for these injuries: Patrick Munn, also known as Mono. He cited provocation and self defence and was not charged. Mr Kan, an upright and respectable citizen, backed up his apprentice's testimony.

Years later, Patrick Munn is said to have gone on a spiritual pilgrimage to Japan, and what became of him is a mystery. Mr Kan died in the late 1940s, and some members of the city's oriental community believed he was a rogue Ninja who settled in Liverpool after fleeing Japan in the 1890s, because he murdered a man who violated his sister. There were rumours that he had been involved with the mysterious Ninja slaying of a man in Liverpool in the 1930s.

SOAP SALLY

This story is about one of the strangest people in the history of Liverpool's folklore. Some called her 'Soap Sally', others knew her as 'Dirty Mary', or the 'Dog Lady', because she often gave butcher's bones to any dog she came across, and the grateful animals would trail behind her in packs.

Soap Sally was rarely spotted during the daytime, but once twilight fell, she would invariably make her appearance. She was mostly seen around the Lime Street, London Road and Seymour Street areas, but there were also reported sightings of her as far afield as Wavertree, Kensington and Old Swan. She wore a silk headscarf tied tightly under her chin and a long, grubby-looking coat, baggy tights and quaint black buckled shoes. She would carry a small basket of soap, pegs and other items for sale.

Her sinister reputation was primarily due to her appearance. She was about six feet in height and had a pointed chin and a prominent aquiline nose. Her thick bushy eyebrows met in the middle, shading her piercing dark eyes. She obviously never put the soap she sold to use on herself, because she was filthy and malodorous, yet, her face was always plastered in thick make-up, and some thought Soap Sally was actually a man in drag.

In the late 1950s, Patricia Campbell, a twelve-year-old from Bootle, decided to leave home because her parents were constantly arguing. She delved into her mother's purse, took some money to pay for the bus fare, and decided to travel to Liverpool, where her best friend Susan Saunders lived, somewhere off Cambridge Street. She arrived at Lime Street and went in search of her friend, but was unable to find her. She asked everyone, but no one had heard of the girl. She began to panic and started wandering about aimlessly. She considered returning home, but felt her quarrelsome parents would be livid if she went back, and so dismissed the idea. Darkness was falling and Lime Street was not a suitable place for a young girl. Pat was gazing up at the statue of the naked man over Lewis's, when a cold clammy hand suddenly covered her eyes. "Ooh, Don't look at that, young miss," said a strange voice.

Pat let out a stifled squeal. When the rough foul-smelling hands were removed, she looked up to see a lanky woman stooping over her. It was Soap Sally, though she did not introduce herself, but grabbed her by the hand, and started walking her towards Copperas Hill. Pat's mind was working overtime to find a way to escape from the old crone's clutches. "There's a policeman!" she shouted, and pointed across the road.

Soap Sally looked across, no policeman was in sight. Pat

used the opportunity to break free and without looking back, ran like fury up Lime Street, until she had a 'stitch' in her side. She shuddered at the memory of the woman who had tried to grab her and whose pungent body odour still assailed her nostrils. Then an unusual sight diverted her attention: a dazzling advertisement on a hoarding on the corner of London Road, of a girl on a swing advertising 'Full Swing Lemonade'. As Pat stood mesmerised by the illuminated advert, Soap Sally caught up with her and struck again, only this time she grabbed the girl's arm and Pat could not break free. Sally pulled what looked like a knife out of her covered basket, and threatened, "You'll never see your mummy or daddy again if you make a sound." She bared her yellow teeth at Pat, who felt as if her legs were starting to buckle. She started to cry.

As Sally turned to go up Lord Nelson Street, she came to a sudden halt. Coming towards her was Jimmy Fleet, a teddy boy and a real hard-knock from the Bullring tenements. He took one look at Soap Sally and little Pat, and in one movement, produced a flick-knife and clicked it open. Sally swore at him and pushed Pat forwards. Jimmy beckoned for the crying girl to come to him and he positioned himself in front of her. Sally took out a carving knife from her basket and brandished it at the youth for a moment, then thought better of it and turned and fled in disappointed rage. As she ran away, she moved like a man, and displayed her prominent masculine calf muscles.

In an uncharacteristically chivalrous gesture, Jimmy took Pat to the police station, from where she was returned to her parents. The police made enquiries, and visited the house on Seymour Street, said to be Soap Sally's home, but got no reply. Through the front window, all they could see was a Yorkshire terrier looking back at them from a basket. A forced entry was made, but the place was deserted – even the terrier turned out to be stuffed. So too was a budgie they found. The neighbours told all sorts of wild stories, including claims that the soap which Sally sold contained fat made from human bodies!

A month after her terrifying encounter, Pat woke up at half-past three in the morning to tapping on her bedroom window. When she looked out, there on the pavement was Soap Sally cackling and throwing stones up at her. She pointed a grubby finger at the petrified girl, then made a cut throat gesture with her finger across her neck, then ran off. Maybe it was a nightmare, but to Pat it seemed all too real and some people say that Soap Sally's ghost still walks the streets of Liverpool.

THE BOAR'S HEAD

On Christmas Eve, 1805, a stagecoach was due to leave Wavertree, Liverpool, for a four-day journey to London. It was supposed to have left four days earlier, but heavy snowstorms had delayed its departure. It was six o'clock and the ten passengers were enjoying their breakfast at the Lamb, which catered for travellers in Wavertree. They were seated at a large table, eating and drinking heartily before departing on their arduous journey. John Ponsonby, an elderly corpulent businessman, sat with his substantial back to the open fire, blocking off the warmth from all the others. He had a voracious appetite, and was cramming mutton, roast potatoes and peas into his mouth, as if this were his last meal on earth. He stated his business intentions as he chewed enormous mouthsful of food.

One of the travellers had been taken ill, so there was a

vacant seat in the coach. That same morning, a young troublemaker named Robert Matty, was released from the lock-up, a small local gaol which still stands today near Wavertree's Picton Clock. Matty had spent the night there for being drunk and disorderly and his aunt, tired of his behaviour, marched him up to Billy Rigg, the landlord of the Lamb, and paid the fare to have him taken to London, where his Uncle Jack worked. She hoped that he would employ him and that Matty would settle down at last.

Matty was allotted the vacant seat on the coach, and at half-past-six, all was ready, and the ten travellers climbed aboard. The four poorest passengers sat outside on special roof seats, open to the elements. No sooner had the stagecoach trundled off down what is now Childwall Valley Road, than heavy snow started to fall once more, but the four powerful horses battled on as the coachman cracked this whip. When the coach had passed Knutsford, later that day, a real blizzard had begun to rage. As Mr Ponsonby swigged from his brandy flask, young Matty snatched it from him and took a swig himself. The coach slowed down as the horses laboured through ever deeper snowdrifts and the coachman called for people to help him shovel a path through the snow and ice, but the only man to respond was Lancashire preacher, Samuel Birchall, who shook his head in disgust at the other selfish passengers. "Many can help one, but one can't help many," he said sanctimoniously, but his fellow travelling companions just ignored him and the four shivering passengers from the coach roof barged past him and squeezed into the vehicle's slightly warmer interior. The preacher and the coachman battled against the worsening blizzard, shovelling furiously; if they could not clear a path, the coach would be snow-bound.

Young Matty leant out of the window and pointed at

something in the distance. "Look, there's a light!" he cried. The grey outline of a cottage, with a stable next to it, could just be discerned a short distance away. Lights were burning inside and the coachman decided to try and take the stagecoach over to the cottage, where the owner might allow him to shelter the horses until the weather improved.

The 'cottage' was in fact a large inn and the coachman wiped the snow from the window and peered inside. People inside were eating, drinking and dancing and a huge welcoming log fire was roaring in the grate. The coachman entered with Reverend Birchall and young Matty, and they approached the counter to ask the innkeeper if there was room for them all to stay at the inn. The innkeeper's round, rosy face broke into a broad smile. "Of course, bring them all in!" he said.

The travellers were soon seated with the other guests at a huge table. Mr Ponsonby drooled as a silver platter bearing a boar's head, with an apple in its mouth, appeared from the kitchen, surrounded by enormous roast potatoes and swimming in gravy and peas. Fine malt liquor, rum and stout was served, all on the house. The guests were overjoyed. They had faced the prospect of being marooned all night in the freezing blizzard, and now, here they were in the middle of a party! In the corner, a buxom woman sat on young Matty's knee and started to kiss and flirt with him. The preacher, meanwhile, sat by the fire watching the proceedings. When the clock chimed midnight, he said, "Do you all realise that it is now Christmas?" Everyone fell silent. Taking a small Bible from his haversack, he said, "I will now read St Matthew's account of the birth of Jesus."

At that moment, the innkeeper started to snarl, and shouted, "No!" and Matty screamed, because the girl he had been kissing had somehow changed into an old hag. Then the boar's head opened its mouth wide, releasing the apple. Its piggy eyes fixed on the preacher. "Throw that book in the fire!" it ordered.

Meanwhile, old Ponsonby had stopped his feeding frenzy, as his face contorted and he clawed at his chest in agony. The shock of seeing the talking boar's head had brought on a heart attack. Within seconds, his body crumpled, as he fell dead to the floor, upon which the boar's head roared with laughter. Dust fell from the oak beams and the stone floor shook. The log fire spat out sparks and tongues of flame, and most of the travellers made a sharp beeline for the door. As two of Mr Ponsonby's friends dragged his swollen body from under the table, a partly-chewed potato shot from his mouth. They dropped him unceremoniously and careered through the door in terror.

The preacher had realised that the inn was a cruel illusion created by the Devil and when Matty screamed because the shrivelled-up harridan would not let go of him, he prised him loose from her bony fingers. The two men backed out of the inn and hastily stumbled through the snow drifts to the coach.

As the last passenger, Henry Long, was scrambling into the coach, he took one last look at the inn. A mound of gold coins had suddenly appeared in the hallway, and being desperately poor, he ran in to grab some of the glittering currency. But, as soon as crossed the threshold, the heavy oaken doors slammed shut behind him, trapping him inside. The entire inn was then swallowed up as the ground quaked. Turning their backs on the evil place, and the blizzard having now abated somewhat, the survivors set off again, trying to make sense of the night's awful events as they were jostled and jolted by the coach, and it lurched onwards over the rutted, snow-covered roads.

When they finally arrived at Kidsgrove, they were all still in a state of shock and all signed affidavits explaining Mr Ponsonby's death and Henry Long's disappearance … and young Robert Matty? He was so chastened by his experiences, he never misbehaved again!

GREY GHOST

In 1967, Paul, an eighteen-year-old Liverpool teenager, started dating sixteen-year-old Julie, from the Claughton district of Wirral. She was very beautiful, and most of the boys at her school were madly in love with her, but Paul had started seeing her in the summer of 1967, during a school trip to Wales. Julie was quite a demanding girl, used to getting her own way and soon pestered Paul to buy her an engagement ring and other items of jewellery to prove his love. Paul was only an apprentice painter, and already spent almost all his meagre wages on the daily ferry fares to see his girl, as well as taking her out as often as he could.

Paul was the white sheep of a notorious Toxteth family, and between June and August 1967, his three older brothers had broken into a number of tombs in St James's Cemetery. Most of the items stolen were Victorian and Edwardian jewellery, and somewhere along the line, Paul managed to obtain a purloined ring that had been wrenched from the skeletal digit of William Owen, who died around 1860. The cygnet ring, with its blood red stone, found its way on to Julie's slender finger. It only fitted her middle finger, but she loved wearing it, and showed it off to all her friends.

In the September of 1967, when a thick fog blanketed Merseyside, Julie's father was alarmed to hear a frantic hammering on his front door one night. He rushed out to find his daughter with the colour drained from her face and unable to talk, struck dumb with terror. She fought to get past him but he grabbed her wrists, and asked her what the matter was. She managed just one word, 'attacked', as she looked over her shoulder to check no one was following her. Julie and her father then saw a figure emerging from the fog; he wore a tall top hat and seemed grey from head to foot – every part of him monochrome, as if he had stepped out of a black and white film. What really spooked them was the way the figure moved through the low brick wall which surrounded the front garden.

Julie broke free of her father, ran into the house, straight through the lounge and out again via the back door, whilst he froze as he noticed that the apparition had a black hook where his right hand should be. His face was truly terrifying. The eyes were as black as ebony and seemed to be boiling over with a terrible anger. The vision brought a sharp pain to his chest. He staggered into the hallway and slammed the door shut, but immediately something started rapping on the door with a sharp metallic sound that could only be the hook.

When he plucked up enough courage to peer through the curtains in the front room, he could see nothing at all, everything obscured by the thick, swirling fog. Julie did not return that night, but stayed in her friend's house. When she eventually returned the following sunny morning, she told her dad that the top hatted man had followed her up Bidston Road in the fog. At first she thought it was just someone messing about, but then she noticed that the creepy figure made no sound as he walked and looked like a photograph. She ran away from him, but he caught her up and grabbed her hair. She managed to break free and kept running until every fibre in her body ached and she had reached her front door. A week later, the same figure was seen again by Julie's father, as it stood at their garden gate, before evaporating into the air.

Around this time, one of Paul's ex-girlfriends bumped into Julie and took great pleasure in telling her that her ring had been stolen from a crypt. She confronted Paul and his face betrayed his guilt. She flung the ring at him saying she never wanted to see him, or his stolen ring, again. From that time onwards, the ghostly man with the hook never bothered Julie or her family again.

In 1992 I was told that William Owen, the man whose grave had been robbed, had lost his hand in an accident and had had a hook fitted in its place!

STORM IN A TEACUP

Around 1963 or 1964, twenty-year-old Judy was employed in the cannery of Princes Pure Foods, in the city centre, which produced such delights as ox tongue, braised kidneys and pork luncheon meat. The mind-numbing job did not pay well, but as Judy lived with her parents in the overcrowded family home on Peel Street, she had few expenses, and always had enough cash to go out on the town with friends on a Friday and Saturday night. One club she frequented was the world famous Cavern Club in Matthew Street, where the Beatles came to prominence, and this was where she met handsome Nicolas Lasarndt.

The twenty-two-year-old Frenchman was tall and dark and everyone remarked on his striking resemblance to the

French film heart-throb, Alain Delon. He had travelled to Liverpool to be part of the Merseybeat scene, as a so-called beat poet. He was staying at the YMCA, and one Saturday night, after the Cavern was closing, he managed to smuggle Judy into his room. At their first meeting, Judy fell deeply in love with Nicolas, or Nick as she called him; a typical romantic Frenchman, reciting poems to her and buying her flowers and wine. Actually, the flowers had usually been stolen from Abercromby Park and the wine was cheap plonk, but Judy thought he was the man of her dreams.

During her lunch hour one day, Nick visited Judy at work and announced, very publicly, that he had bought her a ring. All her workmates stopped what they were doing and watched with bated breath. Judy felt faint as he produced a novelty key-ring with a miniature flashlight as the fob. Everyone guffawed with laughter, but Judy felt utterly humiliated. Then Nicolas smiled broadly and produced a small velvet-lined box and got down on bended knee. Judy threw her hands to her face in embarrassment as her workmates gasped. In French, he asked if she would marry him. She nodded, crying out, "Yes! Oh, yes!" upon which Nicolas kissed her knuckles and then slipped on the gold band. Everyone patted them on the back and cheered. Nicolas arranged for the wedding to be held in Paris that June, at the church his family attended near Notre Dame. Judy could barely contain herself, and went on a shopping trip with friends to find a wedding gown.

During the lunch break at the factory one day, Mrs Magdalena, an elderly worker, was asked by one of the girls to read the tea leaves in her teacup. The old lady had made some very accurate predictions in the past, using a practice known as 'tasseomancy' in the occult world. She took hold of the cup the girl had been drinking from, swirled the tea around three times, then turned it upside down over the old sink.

"Tap the cup!" she said to the girl, which she did.

Mrs Magdalena then righted it and studied the shapes made by the soggy tea leaves. "Mm ... a man on a motorbike. Oh dear!" she sighed, frowning.

"What? What is it?" asked the girl apprehensively.

"Be very careful crossing the roads, dear," warned Mrs Magdalena. "That's all I can tell you."

A few days later, the girl came into work with a bandaged right hand. She showed it to the supervisor and asked if she could be let off work. She had been crossing Dale Street, when a motorcyclist sped past her, just missing her. The motorcycle's handlebar grazed her, taking the skin off the back of her hand. Everyone was stunned, including Judy. The old woman obviously had special powers, so she asked her to read her tea leaves. She was reluctant at first, but Judy insisted. A pot of Kardomah brand tea was brewed; Judy drank half of it, then Mrs Magdalena took hold of the cup, swirled the tea around three times, and turned it upside down over the old sink. Judy tapped the base of the cup. The pattern formed by the tea leaves was very odd. Clear for everyone to see, was the image of a man with a Van Dyke beard. There was a face close to his – a woman's face. What looked like hands were at her throat. There was also a small round face, a little girl's face in the cup.

"Oh dear!" Mrs Magdalena gasped.

Another two women came over, saw the image, and asked Judy if she knew anyone with such a beard. She could not think of anyone and Mrs Magdalena quickly rinsed the cup and went back to work.

A fortnight before the wedding, Nicolas returned from a three-week stay in Paris and her heart sank when she saw he had grown a Van Dyke beard! Nicolas thought the beard added an air of authenticity to his beat poet image, but Judy inwardly shuddered, but said nothing.

A few days later, she was sitting in the YMCA lounge with Nicolas when in walked a young woman with long black hair. She marched over to them and spat at Nicolas. The globule of saliva landed squarely on his face and he wiped it away in disgust. She then began shouting unintelligible things at him in French. Seething with anger, he leapt up and grabbed her by the throat, squeezing and shaking her so hard her eyes bulged. The girl passed out and Judy started to scream.

Two men who had been playing chess in the lounge tackled Nicolas and managed to prise his hands away from the girl's throat, which was purple and bruised. The police arrived and soon established that the victim was Nicolas's wife of three years. It also came to light that they had a little girl back home in Paris, who was ill and had repeatedly asked for her father, but he was too busy womanising in England to go to her. Judy had to accept that Nicolas was an out and out cad who had thought nothing of committing bigamy. Trying to maintain her self control, she flung the ring back at him, but as soon as she was out of his sight, she cried bitter tears and dejectedly made her way home.

Two Terrifying Exorcisms

The following account was told to me by a Catholic priest when we were discussing the Rites of Exorcism. He maintained that even the holiest person was not immune to possession. Indeed, it was recently claimed that Mother Theresa of Calcutta underwent exorcism shortly before her death. The priest said that the Church frowned upon the undue sensationalism which the media creates when reporting exorcisms, and it was only after retirement that he was able to divulge a couple of his truly amazing cases to me, without bringing down the wrath of the Church upon his head.

In 1956, Ray, a thirteen-year-old Liverpool schoolboy, went to town with his Uncle John. He collected stamps, so his uncle took him to McGoff's, in Moorfields, a shop that specialised in stamps and philately. John bought him a pack of assorted stamps and they left the shop. As they were leaving, John bumped into George Terry a friend he had not seen in years. The two men started chatting and suddenly, Ray tugged on his uncle's sleeve. "What is it, Ray?" asked John, annoyed by his nephew's rudeness.

"Uncle, that man's going to die tonight," he said, indicating George with his eyes.

This naturally caused something of a stir and Ray was reprimanded and told to remain quiet when adults were having a conversation. His uncle apologised to his friend, but later that night, John was drinking in his local – the Swan Vaults, on Conway Street in Everton, when he heard some shocking news. That evening, George Terry, having finished his tea, relaxed into his armchair, never to get up again. John thought about the morbid prediction Ray had made earlier in Moorfields and asked him how he had known George would die. "I get this smell ... a sweet sickly smell," explained Ray. "I think it's the smell of some stuff they embalm bodies with, Uncle John."

On the following day, Ray's eldest sister, Janet, visited the family, bringing her nine-month-old baby son. Ray asked if he could hold the baby, and Janet let him, but warned him to be very careful. Ray started rocking the baby in front of the fireplace, when suddenly, as the family was smiling at him, the babe started babbling. He was clearly heard to say, "Hello Janet," before starting to cry. Everyone recoiled with surprise.

"Did you hear that?" gasped Janet.

"I did that!" said Ray, upon which his sister snatched the baby back, and everyone felt very uneasy. It had not been ventriloquism; the baby had spoken clearly in a low voice.

On the Monday morning, Ray's mother went into his bedroom to get him up for school, when she came upon a horrible sight. Ray was lying on his bed in his pyjamas, with a thick viscous brown liquid oozing from his mouth, ears and eyes. It smelt utterly vile. She frantically called her sister to the room and they used towels to wipe away the foul liquid, but it kept welling up as fast as they cleared it. They tried to wake him, fearful that he might choke, but he could not be roused. A doctor was called, and he admitted that he had never seen anything like the brown matter that had now swamped Ray and most of the bed.

All of a sudden, the boy started talking in a language that the doctor recognised as Swahili, having been raised in Kenya. Translating for the benefit of Ray's mother and aunt, he said that he was muttering something about evil spirits. Ray's mother was so alarmed by the state of her child, that the doctor suggested calling a priest. As they were Catholic, they sent for their local priest, Father Elliot, who duly turned up and found the boy, now completely swamped in the sticky brown liquid, levitating slowly off the bed, screaming in terror. Father Elliot, Ray's mother and aunt and a neighbour, frantically tried to pull him back down, but they were all almost lifted off their feet by the powerful force that was making Ray float. He rose to the ceiling, where he left a dark stain from the revolting material issuing from his mouth. Then the force that was gripping him suddenly released him and he plunged back on to the bed.

Then, in a raspy voice, unlike his own, Ray began to speak, "We're taking the woman at Number forty-nine to Hell!" he croaked. Living at that house was Katie Walsh, who that night died of a thrombosis in her sleep.

The priest decided to carry out the Rites of Exorcism on the boy using bell, book and candle and allegedly expelled five evil spirits, including the spirit of an Edwardian murderer. Ray returned to normality, and the priest visited him regularly for years, just to ensure that all was well. The boy was never possessed again.

The second exorcism had been related to the priest by his uncle and began in 1922, when the father of a family of five living on Livingston Drive contacted a Father Williams and told him that their house was being haunted by a terrifying apparition. The priest was a little sceptical at first, but went along to the house and witnessed the violent poltergeist activity at first hand. Knives flew out of a cutlery drawer and stabbed at his palms, and another time hot lumps of coal flew out of the fire, showering him and the family. An older priest soon arrived and advised the family to pack their bags and stay with relations until the problem could be sorted out. They needed little persuasion and went to stay in Kirkdale, but were so distraught the local parish priest had to counsel them.

Meanwhile, the supernatural activity at the abandoned house on Livingston Drive intensified. Yellowish acrid vapours rose from the carpets, and grotesque leering faces appeared on the walls in the form of damp stains. An investigator from a psychical research society fled the house after seeing a demonic head appear in the flames of the fire. The head spat out something deeply personal, only understood by the man, which affected him so severely that he never returned. In the cellar, the floor would at times seem to give way and the cries of tormented souls could be heard. Holy water was liberally splashed around, but it only seemed to provoke the chilling hysterical laughter. A neighbour who once dared to venture into the house to see what all the fuss was about, fled when a six-inch long shiny black beetle came scrabbling after him down the hallway. He was in such a hurry to get out, that he twisted his ankle on the front step.

An elderly nun from a convent in Hope Street, who had dealt with visitations of the Devil, and was familiar with his crafty shenanigans, was asked to help. Armed with a rosary, a Bible, a silver crucifix and, of course, her faith, which was probably much stronger than the average cleric's, she set off for Livingston Drive. As the car she was travelling in sped down Windsor Street, a swarm of hornets attacked it, and the driver had to veer off down Northumberland Street to escape. The nun immediately suspected that the hornets were an obstacle sent by Satan to delay her. Then, as the old car was travelling up Park Road, the chassis started to vibrate violently, and the driver complained that something was wrong with the steering. The nun ordered him to drive on and whispered a series of prayers; as she did so, the car gradually stopped vibrating.

On Aigburth Road, a beautiful gleaming yellow Bentley

screeched to a halt in front of them. Two beautiful young women were in the Bentley, and the one who was driving sounded her horn and waved frantically at the driver of the nun's car. The driver stopped the car and asked what the trouble was, and seemed entranced by the two women as they giggled and pointed to the Bentley's bonnet. The nun got out and surveyed the pair, who simply ignored her. She believed them to be another diabolical illusion, conjured up to hinder and frustrate her attempts to reach her destination. She urged the driver to take her there immediately, but by now the two women were taking off his jacket and coaxing him to fix the Bentley's engine.

The nun flagged down another vehicle and asked the driver to take her to Livingston Drive. He willingly agreed but, for some reason, was unable to find the street. He had been reared in South Liverpool and knew the area well, but seemed confused and apologised to the nun. So she left the car and located the house on foot. Her chauffeur later reported that, as soon as the nun had left, the two women drove off without saying another word.

What happened next is not too clear, but years later, one of the priests recalled that the nun had gone down into the cellar reciting, "Though I walk through the valley of the shadow of death, I will fear no evil, for thou art with me". Five minutes later, a shadowy entity, about thirty feet in length, rose out of the cellar and passed through the top of the house. Two bright points of light looked like eyes, and it faded away as it drifted over towards the local park, before vanishing. The nun allegedly claimed that it had been one of the fallen angels, cast down on to the earth with Lucifer many years ago and awakened by someone in the neighbourhood who had been dabbling with the occult.

NIGHT FERRY

In June 1901, Stephen Donnelly, a young Cambridge undergraduate, was on vacation down in Devon at a small cottage in Exmouth. One night, at around twelve o'clock, he was reading in bed and gradually started to feel drowsy. He turned off the oil lamp and sank into a deep, dreamless sleep. He was awakened some time later by a voice somewhere nearby. The bedroom was pitch black because the heavy drapes had been tightly drawn. Donnelly froze as he heard the words, "Go down to the ferry." He was slowly reaching for the bedside clock, ready to throw it at the intruder, when the voice spoke again, "Go down to the ferry, the boatman awaits."

Donnelly bolted out of bed and ran to the window, almost ripping down the curtains as he flung them apart. Moonlight flooded the empty room. Not a soul was to be seen. He lit the oil lamp and sat uneasily on the bed digesting what he had heard. After a while he tried to sleep again, only this time he felt more comfortable leaving the lamp lit. He exhaled in relief, adjusted his pillow, and closed his eyes. Moments later, the disembodied voice spoke again.

"Go down to the ferry, the boatman awaits," it said, this time far more insistently.

Donnelly snapped open his eyes and sat up in one reflexive movement. He looked about; still nobody there. Goosebumps erupted all over his skin. "Who are you?" he asked. There was no reply, so he got fully dressed, and as he was unable to sleep, decided to go for a walk down to the River Exe, which was not too far away. When he reached the ferry's small landing stage, he saw the dark hulking shape of a boat, barely visible through the thick mist suspended like a blanket over the river. Suddenly, a loud voice boomed out, "Are you Donnelly?"

Out of the swirling mist on the pier walked a man with a grey beard – the ferryman, Mr Thorne, who lived across the River Exe at a place on the riverfront called Starcross. Donnelly was puzzled when he said that he had been roused from his sleep by a frantic voice outside his hut crying, "Mr Donnelly is waiting to be taken from across the river. A man's life depends on this!" Yet when he got outside he saw only the ghostly night vapours, tracing the sinuous contours of the river. He assumed that someone on a passing boat had shouted the command, but he heard it again shortly afterwards, so he had come across the river to see if a Mr Donnelly was indeed waiting.

As Donnelly boarded the ferry, he told the ferryman about the voice bidding him to cross the river. At the Starcross pier, Mr Thorne departed, saying that he intended to get some sleep for an early rise the next morning and he bid the student goodnight. Left alone, Stephen Donnelly ended up walking through the night, now separated from his home by the river. At around 1am, the voice spoke again, this time more forcefully: "Go north to Exeter," it commanded.

That meant walking some five miles, but Donnelly obeyed, fascinated by the disembodied voice. He walked on until the early summer dawn paled the sky, eventually coming to a hotel, where he stopped to have breakfast. The place was unusually busy, as the assizes were being held at the nearby court. He learned that a carpenter, originally from Liverpool, had been arraigned on a capital charge, and was expected to be sentenced to hang, so people had come from miles around to pack into the gallery. On a whim, Donnelly also decided to go to the court.

The carpenter, a man named Jim Ashton, had been accused of killing a woman. All the evidence was circumstantial, but conviction seemed inevitable. If only he could find a witness to put him somewhere else at the time of the murder, he would escape the hangman's noose, but there was not even an opening for the defence, and the judge had his black cap at the ready.

All of a sudden, Stephen Donnelly recognised the accused man and recalled that on the date of the murder, Jim Ashton had been the carpenter who had mended the sash-line of the cottage window where he was staying. He stood up and testified to the court, and the judge asked if he had any proof that Ashton had been there. Donnelly thought hard – there must be something.

"Yes! wait a moment ..." he cried jubilantly, pulling a small brown object from his pocket. "This is the carpenter's pencil I borrowed from Mr Ashton, to sign the invoice for the mended window. I forgot to give it back and it ended up in my pocket."

He also remembered that he had a copy of the invoice back at the cottage. When the new evidence was confirmed, the jury returned a verdict of not guilty and Jim Ashton was aquitted and released. Donnelly told him the story about the phantom voice and the Liverpool carpenter said, "Aye, I believe you. You heard my guardian angel." Ashton explained that something benevolent had been looking after him ever since he became an orphan in Liverpool many years ago. Mr Donnelly, and Mr Thorne the ferryman, signed an affidavit confirming that they had both heard the voice which had saved a man from the gallows.

WARNING AT THE ALTAR

In the year 1879, moderately successful businessman John Pickavance, met twenty-year-old Martha at a ball in Knotty Ash. Martha Brewster was a servant employed by the Warbrick family and, as a special treat, she had been given the night off to attend the ball with the Warbricks' youngest daughter, Emily, who was just sixteen. John Pickavance, who was about forty-five, and originally from Salford, approached Martha, who was said to have been exceptionally beautiful with a personality to match. Pickavance was balding, rather stout, and yet had a certain way with the opposite sex. He took hold of the shy servant's hand, kissed it, and asked if she would care to dance. Martha accepted and Emily Warbrick watched them waltz away. Mr Pickavance could not resist constantly embracing her and in the end, Emily had to literally wrench the girl out of his lustful arms.

Back at the Warbricks' house, Martha seemed to be in a dream, and told Emily and her older sisters that she had agreed to meet John Pickavance in a fortnight's time, on her next night off. However, on the following morning, Pickavance called at the Warbricks' house, and Martha answered the door in her servant's uniform. He thrust a bouquet of scarlet roses at her and sank to his knees, kissing her hand and proclaiming his love for her. Martha blushed as Mrs Warbrick and her three daughters came down to see what all the fuss was about and were astonished to see Mr Pickavance with his arms round her skirts, howling like a baby, and declaring that he had not experienced such an intense love since he was a boy. Being rather overweight and out of shape, he had difficulty getting back to his feet, and the Warbrick girls had to help him up.

When he had left, Martha wandered about in a dreamy daze. Mrs Warbrick was scandalised by the unseemly carryings on, but the Warbrick girls took Martha into the kitchen and poured her a glass of claret in celebration, delighted by the romance and excitedly predicting that it would not be long before wedding bells were ringing.

A fortnight later, Martha met her passionate admirer at another ball. During the evening, John Pickavance began anxiously scrutinising the dance floor. He complained that he had lost a silver locket which was of sentimental value, but the floor was so crowded and dimly lit, he was unable to find it. By pure chance, Martha did find the locket, and instead of immediately handing it to Pickavance, she went to powder her nose and opened it. Inside was a miniature portrait – an exact double of herself! She stared at it long and hard. After a time she composed herself and went back into the dance hall and pretended to find the locket, upon which John Pickavance snatched it from her. Martha asked him what was in it and he replied, rather shiftly, "Nothing, nothing, my dear."

Martha soon forgot the locket incident and was courted for almost six months, until the relationship progressed to the stage where Pickavance proposed and she accepted. The wedding was due to take place at St John the Evangelist's Church, in Knotty Ash, but John Pickavance held a wild stag party the night before, and was so sick on the following morning, that he was half an hour late. Martha waited and waited, becoming more and more fretful with each passing minute, surrounded by anxious friends and relatives. The young maid started to cry, and her aunt tried to comfort her, "There! There! Don't you fret, he'll be ..." but she stopped mid-sentence when she suddenly noticed the colour draining from Martha's face.

A thin woman, wearing a white hood, stepped forward from the crowd and approached her, though it seemed that no one else could see her. She was clad in a burial shroud and had dark circles around her sunken eyes. She smiled at Martha, who watched, speechless, as she pulled the shroud away from her neck to reveal a dark gaping slit.

"He killed me! Wed him not," she whispered.

Martha Brewster screamed and ran out of that church, passing a bewildered John Pickavance as he was climbing out of a hansom cab. Nobody else saw the ghost, but when the jilted John Pickavance heard what had transpired, he withdrew all his money from his bank and left Liverpool.

We know that Mrs Matilda Pickavance had gone missing from her home in Manchester ten years before, and that her body was never found. Had John Pickavance murdered her? and had her spirit returned from the grave to warn Martha Brewster?

THE WEREWOLVES
OF COUNTY FERMANAGH

Werewolves are usually imagined to be people who have turned into wolves through some supernatural physiological process, but the origins of the tale hint that the creatures of the night are actually permanent wolf-like animals. The myth suggests that the people they bite do transform into humanoid versions of wolves (and not always when the moon is full) for a defined period of time, before reverting back to their original selves. Surely there is no hard evidence for such metamorphoses?

Well, there are a surprising number of testimonies from prominent and honest people, spanning from ancient times to the present day. For example, in the fifteenth century, Pierre Mamor, the Rector of a French university, wrote extensively on the werewolf from contemporary sightings and encounters, including the disturbing, well-witnessed account of a Lorraine peasant, who watched in horrified disbelief as her farmer husband clutched at his throat while he sat at the table, ready to eat. He started to vomit, and slowly, a small child's arm emerged from his mouth. Witnesses said the farmer had turned into a wolf the night before and had devoured a child. A priest later exorcised the farmer, and claimed that werewolves were demonic entities that could possess people and turn them into blood-hungry beasts. History abounds with such reports, ranging from the terrifying Beast of Gevaudan, an unknown species of wolf that killed men, women and children in eighteenth century France, to the so-called mysterious 'big cats' of England, such as the Beast of Bodmin and the Surrey Puma.

The following strange story comes from three separate sources: a Liverpool soldier who served in Northern Ireland in the 1970s, an old book on Irish folklore and a few clippings from the Irish press.

The land along the border of County Fermanagh in Northern Ireland is lonely and wild, consisting mostly of mountain, lake and bog, dotted here and there with small villages and hamlets. The mist rolls back and forth across a bleak but beautiful landscape, lingering in the hollows and fashioning weird shapes out of ancient standing stones. The region is famous for its caves and potholes, and there are many deep and still unfathomed caverns. For hundreds of years, people have heard strange beasts in these caverns. From time to time, people claim to have been lost in such places and carried away to the dark realms below, by the so-called werewolves of Fermanagh.

In 1978, a unit of nine soldiers, including one from Liverpool, was on patrol in this part of County Fermanagh. At 3am, they made camp in a wooded area overlooking a farm by the light of a full moon. The soldiers cursed such nights, when the moonlight showed them up. At 3.15am, they were startled by what sounded like a diabolical chorus of wolves, coming from the direction of the mountains. The commander of the unit dismissed the howls as late night revellers, but the soldiers weren't so sure. Whoever the howlers were, they were getting closer and soon they saw four dark shapes materialise on a hilltop, silhouetted against the full moon, like wolves, but twice the size. The commander reasoned that the animals only looked bigger because they were on the horizon, but one of his men had a look at the creatures through infra red binoculars. They were enormous – about seven feet in length – and seemed to be working as a pack, as they slowly surrounded a bull in the corner of a field. Cows and bulls sleep standing up and are pretty insensible when they are asleep. The unit watched in fascination as the animals simultaneously attacked the unsuspecting bull, and the sounds of its squeals, together with the snarls and roars of the wolf-like animals, had the soldiers nervously reaching for their rifles. Three of them escaped, each dragging off one of the bull's muscular legs.

The soldiers then watched in awe as the bull's massive twitching torso was hauled up the hillside by one of the predators. This creature looked silvery grey in the moonlight, whereas the other three were jet black. At one point, it suddenly stopped to tear out the bull's throat, probably to make it easier to drag in a lifeless state.

As soon as the four animals had slunk silently over the hilltop, the commander set off for the spot where the attack had taken place, accompanied by three soldiers. They found a solitary leg and part of the bull's hind quarters, the nerves of which were still twitching. They were inspecting the huge clawmarks in the flesh and the trail of blood, when the large grey wolf-like animal made a reappearance. It pounded towards the four men, snarling ferociously, with fangs exposed and blood smeared around its jaws. The commander gave orders to fire, and two of the soldiers aimed their SLR rifles at the beast and took aim. In two seconds, eighty rounds had found their target, the animal's body twisted and leapt high into the air as the bullets ripped through it. Then it rolled down the hillside, yelping, until the body juddered to a halt about twenty-five feet away from the soldiers. It looked like a wolf, but it was far far bigger, with exceptionally long muscular hind legs. Its incisor fangs were six inches long.

The soldiers beat a swift retreat as more of the creatures streamed down the hillside, encircling the body of their fallen pack member. Watching cautiously, the commander told his men to hold their fire, as their weapons had already blown the reconnaissance patrol's cover. The creatures proceeded to drag the massive limp form up the hillside. At first light, the soldiers followed the trail of blood and discovered that it led into a vast system of mountain caves. A group of Canadian wildlife experts investigated the sightings and tracks left by the animals and confirmed that a species of unknown creature was at large in the area.

In 1983, two soldiers were allegedly attacked by a creature in County Fermanagh. One of them showed the claw marks which the animal had made in his flak jacket. Both soldiers described the dangerous beast as a very large wolf, which ran off, seemingly wounded.

WHERE'S ALICE?

My research is featured on a number of Internet websites, so I get a regular stream of emails from people all over the world, who tell me they enjoy my stories and often send me accounts of their own strange experiences. The following tale is from a man named Ryan who was born in Liverpool in 1979. When he was two, Ryan's family emigrated to Allentown, Pennsylvania, and he now lives in Orange County, California. The story begins in 1995.

Ryan was something of a loner. At sixteen, he had a small number of friends at his high school, but outside the school gates, he was a deeply lonely fellow. His parents and two older sisters were always urging him to unplug his PC and get out and play sports like other teenagers, but Ryan was not interested in sport. He liked tossing a basketball into his slamdunk in the yard now and then, but he was more of a thinker. He read a lot, and was especially keen on books by Ray Bradbury. But Ryan had another avid interest – a girl called Bethany who lived down the street. Bethany was a shapely girl with long straight strawberry-blonde hair, a peaches and cream complexion and a pair of smouldering brown eyes which set many male hearts in the neighbourhood aflutter. She was loved by everyone it seemed, from the garbage men to the local doctor. Ryan had never made it clear that he was interested in her, but whenever she walked to school, he would loiter either a street behind, or a street ahead. To talk to her was unthinkable.

One Valentine's Day he decided to do something to rectify this frustrating state of affairs and sent Bethany an expensive, heavily-embroidered, Valentine's card, and unwisely, and against tradition, signed his name on it. On the morning of 14 February 1995, he was making his way to school, when a voice behind him asked, "Are you Ryan?" He spun round. It was Bethany, and she stood with a giant of a boy named Todd. In her hand she held Ryan's unmistakable, old-fashioned-looking Valentine. She was grinning wickedly.

"Yep," Ryan replied. He didn't like the way Todd was sneering at him, looking him up and down, no doubt laughing at his clothes, which were not particularly fashionable, but there was nowhere to hide.

"Well, here's your card back. Todd's my Valentine," said Bethany and coldly handed the card back to Ryan, whose heart felt as if it had just been injected with ice.

"Okay," he said in a whisper.

Ryan took the card, folded it and angrily threw it into a litter-bin nearby, as the smug couple walked on. The scales had fallen from his eyes and he now knew that Bethany was cruel and cold; a girl who had delighted in mocking his affection for her. He felt no animosity or feelings of revenge towards Bethany or Todd, he was just thankful in a strange way that he had found her out. He knew in his broken heart that there was someone out there who was right for him. He just had to cross her path, that was all.

Well, nothing much romantic happened in Allentown for most of that year. Then, in October, Ryan and his family moved to another part of the town. The new residence was a very old house which dated back to 1900. From the moment he stepped inside the hall, he felt there was something which he could only describe as magical about it. As the weeks went by, Ryan and his family learned from neighbours that the house was supposedly haunted by a ghostly girl. No one knew the ghost's identity, or anything about the history of the house, except for an old woman named Eleanor, who was currently in hospital after a fall. Ryan's father reassured his three children that all the talk about ghosts was pure nonsense; he had once worked near a graveyard at a factory on nightshifts and had never once seen anything remotely supernatural.

Then, one evening, one of Ryan's sisters said she could smell a sweet scent in her room, and insisted that she had felt something brush past her that felt like a silken veil. Then Ryan's mother was cooking supper late one evening, waiting for her husband to return from work, when she heard a piano playing. Her children could hear it too and were equally spooked. Ryan loved a challenge, and so took his flashlight and decided to investigate the source of the phantom music. He realised it was coming from upstairs, and so he climbed to the top of the house, hesitating outside the attic door. He took a deep breath and pushed the door open. He aimed the beam of the flashlight into the room and swept it about; just junk, but what was that large covered object over in the corner?

The music stopped abruptly. The attic light-bulb was missing, and he could hear the faint voices of his mother and sisters calling him back but he continued anyway. He lifted the large canvas dust-sheet off the object, to reveal an old upright piano, a badly-tuned one, with several dead keys, which could not possibly have been the source of the sweet music he had heard. Ryan suddenly got the intense feeling of being watched, so he backed out of the room, whistling for courage, and closed the door.

He was telling his mother and sisters what he had found, when the front door flew open and they all screamed, but it was only Ryan's father, home from work. "What's up? Why're you all standing in the hall?" he laughed, taking off his coat.

They told him about the discovery in the attic, but he just said, "Oh, that's just been mice in that old piano. Where's my tea? I'm ravenous."

That night, the first of many visitations took place. Ryan was lying in the inky-blackness of his bedroom, trying to get to sleep, when he noticed the strong scent of lavender and knew something was in his room. Then he heard a whisper. "Ryan ..." it started.

His heart skipped a beat. "Go away!" he shouted, his voice muffled as he burrowed in the blankets.

He did not recognise the voice; it was not from either of his sisters. Then it came again: "Don't be scared of me, please. My name is Alice."

"Mom!" Ryan called.

He closed his eyes tight and threw himself out of bed. He clicked on the light to find that the room was empty, but the smell was still lingering.

"Ryan?" came his sister's familiar voice from outside the room. "You okay?" She was sympathetic, because she too felt there was something supernatural at large in the house.

"I dunno ... yeah ... better go back to bed."

She nodded, walked off, then yelled as she bumped into her younger sister, also come to see what the commotion was about. As Ryan was closing his door, he heard one of them whisper, "The ghost must have visited Ryan."

He slept with the light on and woke again at 4am, remembering the disembodied girlish voice. Then he felt something warm – a hand holding his. A soft, small hand clasping his outstretched hand, which was dangling out of bed. "Who's there?" he cried.

No reply came and sleep gradually overtook him as the reassuring pale blue light of dawn crept through the curtains. He had the strangest dream, in which he met a beautiful, very old-fashioned girl named Alice. She had a pretty impish face and long plaited chestnut hair. The dream seemed to go on for hours and hours, and in the midst of it there were glimpses of a strange house that stood on the site of Ryan's house. Stranger still, Ryan was besotted with Alice, and she loved him back and he watched her playing the piano from the attic. When she had finished, she whispered, "My picture is in this piano. When you wake up, go upstairs and you'll find it."

"When I wake up? but I'm not asleep."

"Oh, but you are," Alice told him, and as she kissed him, he awoke. His heart sank; the dream had seemed so real.

At midday, Ryan remembered the girl's words and made his way up to the attic. With sunlight blazing through the skylight, the atmosphere was less tense. He opened the top flap of the old piano and shone his flashlight into its inner workings. There was something down there in the thick mildewed dust, nestling amidst the taut piano wires. Ryan reached down, straining his shoulder until he finally retrieved the object. It was an old framed photograph. His heart skipped a beat. The girl in that photograph was Alice. He raced downstairs and showed it to his parents and sisters, and told them about the vivid dreams. Ryan's father was not convinced, "It's all coincidence. If you believe in dreams you might as well spend your life asleep."

Old Eleanor, the neighbour who could throw some light on the history of the house, came out of hospital later that week, and was being looked after by her niece. Ryan's mother took a bunch of flowers and a box of chocolates round and the photograph from the piano. Eleanor, who was a sweet old lady, responded immediately. "That will be Alice Hadley. My mother told me all about her. She died of a fever in the 1880s. Her mother was very puritanical; kept her from seeing boys and having friends, so she used to play the piano. They took the piano out of the house before it was demolished, then after they built the house you're in now, which stands on the same spot, Alice's piano somehow ended up back in there by a fluke. A man named Raymond Jones lived in your house around 1900, and bought the piano from a second-hand shop and my mother recognised it at once as Alice's. Mr Jones was just a magpie and never played that piano, he just had it put away in the attic with the rest of the junk he hoarded."

Ryan's mother was fascinated and asked Eleanor if she had heard about the ghost. She replied, with a glint in her eye, "Yes, and I swear before Almighty God, I saw Alice looking out of the window one day in your home. I hope I'm not scaring you?"

"No, you're not. I'm intrigued."

Ryan underwent a peculiar change, spending most of his days up in the attic, and sometimes his parents would hear complicated piano pieces, even though their son could not play a note. He would chat at the dinner table about how beautiful and talented Alice was and chillingly forecast that, on the day he died, he would marry her in heaven. Ryan's father was becoming very worried about his son's morbid obsession, and contacted a local Catholic priest one morning on his way to work. The priest visited the family accompanied by a medium, which infuriated Ryan. "Mind your own business!" he bawled at the priest. "Alice isn't some evil spirit! She's my girl!"

The priest was worried that the boy was becoming "obsessed and possessed with Alice" and recommended a cleansing of the house. Ryan's father consented enthusiastically and the procedure took place without Ryan's knowledge, whilst he was at school. That evening, when he returned home, he immediately detected a strange silence in the house. His sisters did not breathe a word as he came in, but his mother had a strange, sad look in her eyes.

Ryan went straight up to the attic, but came down about fifteen minutes later. "She's gone!" he choked. His mother hugged him, as his sisters looked on with morose expressions. "Alice has gone. I don't understand," he cried, pushing his mother away.

"Look, love, the church sent these people ..." she began, but trailed off and shook her head.

Ryan recoiled. "What people?"

"They ... they cleansed the house," she explained.

"Two psychics carried out a sort of exorcism," added one of his sisters, "and made Alice go into the light."

"And who let them in? You, Mom?" Ryan asked, with a look of disgust.

She nodded, "Your Father's idea. He was so worried about you."

"I loved her ..." Ryan cried. "I was *in* love with her. She was all I had and you did this." He ran up to the attic, shouting behind him for everyone to leave him alone.

The ghost of Alice Hadley never did return. Ryan initially threatened to commit suicide, so that he could be reunited with his lost love, but he gradually got over the loss, and later found a living breathing person to love and he eventually married her. He has named one of his children Alice, and strangely enough, that little girl was keen to learn how to play the piano ...

THE ART OF BLACKMAIL

On the night of Saturday, 3 January 1863, the Lord Mayor of Liverpool held a magnificent party at the Concert Hall in Lord Nelson Street. Over two thousand guests, drawn from the high society of the North West, attended the lavish event, the proceeds of which were to go to a charity for the poor of the area. Among the illustrious guests was a very mysterious man who introduced himself as Benjamin Julius, an artist who had frequently been commissioned to paint portraits of the highest people in the land. He was also an exceptionally good raconteur, capturing audiences wherever he went with his sparkling anecdotes and ready wit. He would thrill his listeners with tales of the Prince of Wales, with whom he was acquainted, and from whom he had recently received an invitation to his forthcoming marriage to Princess Alexandra of Denmark.

Later in the evening, Mr Julius flamboyantly struck a Lucifer match, let it burn awhile, then blew it out and used its charred end to swiftly execute a flattering charcoal sketch of one of the female guests on a napkin. Lady Leonora Cunningham was captivated by the artist and subsequently commissioned him to paint her portrait at his attic studio on Falkner Street. With due deference and ceremony, Leonora was ushered up to Julius's studio and he positioned his illustrious subject before the diffuse morning sunlight filtering through the northern window. He worked in a fevered frenzy, with a tortured look of determination to fix the vision of feminine beauty before him to mere canvas.

Incredibly, within a span of eight hours, having barely taken a break, the full-length oil portrait was finished. However, when the exhausted Lady Leonora inspected it, the colour drained from her face, and she had to sit down to compose herself. Instead of the pose she had been meticulously holding all day, she was confronted by a picture of herself inexplicably cradling a baby boy with red curly hair. "What on earth is, is … that?" she gasped, tears welling in her eyes.

"Why, it's young Archie, don't you recognise him? That young son of yours that you're hiding from the world," Mr Julius replied, sombrely, his face betraying no emotion.

She certainly did recognise the red-haired child, he was the celebrated lady's darkest secret, the result of an ill-advised affair with the dashing red-headed Captain Lunt, two years before. Lady Leonora had tried for seven long years to conceive a child by her husband, but had produced no offspring. So when Lord Cunningham discovered that she was pregnant, his suspicions were immediately aroused. Uncovering the affair after some investigation, and realising that his wife was carrying another man's child, he ordered her to rid herself of it, but she desperately wanted to keep the child and refused to take such a painful course of action. To try and avert a scandal as the pregnancy advanced, Lord Cunningham had announced that his wife had recently been taken ill, and was now recuperating in North Wales. When she returned, accompanied by the baby with the tell-tale hair, her husband immediately had the infant placed in an orphanage, away from public inspection, angrily declaring to his wife that the baby was not of his own flesh, and he could therefore never have any affection for it.

Lady Leonora was desperate to know how Mr Julius had found out about her closely guarded secret, and warned him to destroy the portrait at once, or face legal action. Instead of being chastened by the wrath of such an elevated personage, his response was simply to tell her to, "Take it to the courts, Madam! I will drag the sordid secrets of you and your husband out into the open for every newspaper in the country to print!" Lady Leonora therefore had no choice but to purchase the painting for four thousand pounds and she later had it destroyed.

There were many more victims of the devious Mr Julius, including mill owner, George Heap, the proprietor of several Lancashire rice mills. In the August of 1863, Mr Julius cordially welcomed Mr Heap into his studio and asked him to adopt the naturalistic pose of lighting a pipe, as he was an inveterate pipe-smoker. The artist then proceeded to paint his portrait, but when it was finished, his subject gazed at the result in horror. He had indeed been depicted holding a lighted match, but through a window behind him could be seen a very familiar building ablaze – the rice mill which Heap owned in Pownall Square.

Only a few weeks before, that mill had been completely gutted by a mysterious fire, and Heap had received a mammoth insurance payment as a result. To any local person looking at the painting, it would immediately suggest that Heap was responsible for setting fire to his own factory, obviously for financial gain. Indeed, most merchants in Liverpool already suspected this to be the case.

Realising that he had been duped, Heap refused to pay for the scandalous painting, and insisted that it be destroyed at once. Mr Julius was unabashed, as usual, declaring that he had no intention of destroying such a wonderful work of art, and that if he refused to pay for it, he would have to exhibit it privately, to recoup his losses. On hearing this, Heap panicked and realised that he had no choice but to pay an undisclosed sum for the artistic work of blackmail.

An entry in the diary of Lady Leonora Cunningham states that, in 1865, the sinister Benjamin Julius suddenly vanished without trace from the Liverpool scene, leaving his Falkner Street studio deserted. Perhaps he had reached a point where it was impossible for him to dupe any more people in the city without being exposed as a blackmailer, and had gone off to look for more fertile pastures elsewhere. No doubt Lady Leonora was heartily relieved to be rid of her artistic tormentor. As for George Heap, he later remarked, "I am sure that he is the Devil in disguise."

CATCH THE BALL

The ancient megalithic Calder Stones of Calderstones Park, in Liverpool, feature strange carvings of occult symbols and engraved maps of star constellations and spiral galaxies. The stones are thought to belong to the late Neolithic period, but no one is absolutely sure, and the entire area now occupied by the park in which the stones stand, has long been regarded as a mystical site. Could the mysterious background of the park have some bearing on the following tale, which I have pieced together over the years from the memories of some of the older denizens of Wavertree and Woolton?

Around 1953, three thirteen-year-old schoolboys, Kenny, Johnny and Bobby, rendezvoused in Calderstones Park one morning to play cricket in the summer sunshine. Kenny brought along a cricket bat, Johnny produced an old scuffed tennis ball and Bobby's rolled-up jumper would serve as the wicket. During play, Kenny bowled and Johnny hit the ball for six, towards the gnarled, thousand-year-old tree Allerton Oak, whose branches had spread so wide that their enormous weight had to be supported by iron props, like crutches. The ball was fielded by an old white-bearded vagrant who was sitting on a bench near the old tree. The boys yelled at him to throw it back, but the old man just sat there, staring into the park, seemingly oblivious to their cries. The three teenagers ran over and Johnny said, "Give us our ball back!"

Instead of handing over the ball, the man just smiled, and patted the bench besides him. "Sit down a minute, lads. I have a few tales to tell you," he said.

The boys noticed that the old man's rheumy eyes were covered with a pale blue film, as if he had a cataract problem. But there was something strangely compelling about him, so they sat down next to him and listened enthralled as he told them many strange and fabulous tales. Halfway through the storytelling, the old man pointed to the boating lake and said, "The Devil's Swan rides on the water there now and then, and if you see him, someone will die in your family."

The three boys shuddered and glanced nervously at the wildfowl on the lake and then at each other. The man then said something which really excited them. "Did you know that one of you three will be the most famous man in the world one day?" he asked.

Naturally, the first thing the boys wanted to know was which of them he was talking about, and by way of reply, the silvery-haired storyteller held out the grubby old tennis ball. "This will decide!"

"I'd watch him if I were you, he's potty," a park warden advised the boys, as he saw them eagerly trailing after the old man, who was still holding the tennis ball out in front of him, like a divining rod. With everything they had ever been told about not talking to strangers a distant memory, they followed the old vagrant, who, like a latter day pied piper, led them right out of the park and across several roads, to a bridge nearly a mile away, overlooking a railway track on Rose Lane, Mossley Hill.

"Now boys," he said, "listen very carefully. When the train comes, I will throw this ball down the funnel, and the steam will shoot it right up into the air by the time it emerges from the other side of this bridge. Whoever catches it will be the most famous man in the world one day."

To an adult, such an outlandish prediction would have seemed preposterous, but to the lads it was a magical challenge. Presently, the train came thundering down the track, puffing a white plume of steam out of its funnel. The man leaned right over the bridge so that the guard-rail was pressed to his navel, with his left arm holding the tennis ball aloft. As the engine arrived below him, he was engulfed in a dense cloud of smoke and steam, and through all the hissing and chugging, the boys could hear him cry, "Bull's eye!"

The locomotive rattled the bridge beneath their feet and they watched the steam erupt from the other side. Just as the old man had predicted, the tennis ball shot skywards, then slowed and came falling back to earth, propelled on a curved trajectory by a sudden gust of wind. Being the most competitive, Kenny pushed his friends to the ground in the scramble to catch the ball, and focused hard as he tried to gauge where it would land, but it slipped through his hands and Johnny just managed to catch it before it hit the ground. He jumped up and down, waving the scruffy tennis ball in triumph. He turned to show it to the old man, but he had gone. They searched the area around the bridge, but he was nowhere to be found.

"The whole thing's stupid, anyway," Bobby told Johnny. "He was having us on ... how could you be the most famous man in the world? You should be so lucky, you skinny little whipper snapper!"

"Yeah! He was just a daft old man, like that parkie said," agreed a sour-faced Kenny. "All that Devil's swan rubbish!"

"Well I won, anyway," said Johnny, philosophically.

"Race you back to the park," said Bobby. "Last one there's a sissy!"

And so Bobby Smith, Kenny Greene and Johnny Lennon ran away from the bridge and back to the park and their game of cricket. The rest, as they say, is history.

THE MYSTERY

I was given this story many years ago by an old blind woman from Wavertree. Her name was Molly, and the tale she told begins on the snowy Victorian winter afternoon of Sunday, 23 December 1894, when a poverty-stricken nine-year-old girl with the quaint name of Rosie Sparks, left her crumbling home on Cow Lane, which is now Prince Alfred Road, and went out to play in the snow with Chip, her mongrel dog. To Rosie's delight, a crunchy carpet of snow had completely covered the cobbles on Cow Lane, transforming her normally dismal playground, into a winter wonderland. She began making a snowman, rolling a ball of snow round and round until it was the size of a barrel. She was so completely taken up with the task, she was oblivious to the biting cold, and stood on the snow in her bare feet, patting it with her thin, mittenless hands.

In the distance stood a huge old mansion called the Grange, set in about a hundred acres of private land. It was a spooky-looking house, surrounded by gnarled trees, whose bare skeletons rattled and scraped at the windows on this cold December day, blown by the chill winter winds. Crooked old Walter Tregeagle roamed the grounds, carrying an old sword and a blunderbuss. A type of gamekeeper cum watchman, he could be very brutal to any trespassers found on the land, be they men, women or children.

The Grange had been the residence of Samuel Graves, a merchant, until his death in 1873, but was now home to a reclusive and rather sinister individual. No one knew his name and very few ever caught so much as a glimpse of him. Many wild rumours circulated, some claiming he had shunned the world after being jilted by his fiancée, others that he was no longer able to live in society, because he was severely disfigured. Gossip was rife, but nobody really knew anything definite, but on this wintry afternoon, Rosie Sparks was destined to find out the truth.

She was so engrossed in building her snowman that she didn't notice that Chip had gone missing until she had finished it. She went home to look for him, but he wasn't there. She looked everywhere. Then a lad named Topper Murphy, so called because he wore a battered old top hat, said he had seen Chip chase a cat through the railings of the entrance gate to the Grange. They ran up to the gate, and the Rosie shouted for her dog, but he didn't turn up. The house and gardens looked so beautiful in the snow that she decided to risk climbing over the gate. Topper helped her, but was too afraid of old Mr Tregeagle to follow. "I'll wait here," he said, anxious that he might appear at any moment.

Rosie was cautiously threading her way through the trees and snow-covered hedges, when a large heavy snow cloud drifted over the estate, darkening the skies and bringing with it an oppressive gloom. She shivered as the pretty scene was transformed into something altogether more alarming. She crouched lower and kept her eyes peeled for

Chip, not even daring to whisper his name now that she was actually inside the gates – then she froze as she felt something sharp and ice-cold brush the nape of her neck.

Full of foreboding, she heard a bronchial cackle behind her and slowly turned to see the dreaded gamekeeper, Walter Tregeagle. He held a long sword which he pointed menacingly at Rosie, and he was dressed in a faded scarlet British Army tunic. On his head he wore a ridiculously tall black military hat called a shako. Tregeagle was a veteran of the Crimean War of 1855. Almost forty years had passed since the hostilities had ceased, but his mind had never recovered from the horrors of war. With twisted lips he snarled at poor Rosie. "You're for it now, young miss," he said and placed the blade of the sword against the centre parting of her hair. "I'm going to slice you right down the middle!" And with a wicked smile, he lifted the sword, ready to strike.

Overcome with terror, and frozen to the marrow, the child passed out. She landed face down in the snow, and as she fell, Chip came bounding out of nowhere and started to snap at the gamekeeper's boots. Tregeagle swung the sword about furiously, missing the mongrel dog by inches. With his floppy ears pressed flat against his head in fear, Chip stood his ground between the demented old soldier and his mistress. In the nick of time, a pair of well-shod feet came crunching through the snow, and a well-spoken voice called out, "Mr Tregeagle! Mr Tregeagle! Stop that at once! Leave the poor child alone!"

The effect of the voice was electric – Tregeagle dropped the sword, straightened himself up and saluted. The man who had brought about this astonishing effect was wearing a bowler hat and a long black coat, and had a thick, woolly scarf wrapped around his face, so that only his eyes could be seen. He ordered Tregeagle to carry Rosie Sparks up to the mansion, where she was given a glass of warm milk laced with rum. When she revived, she jolted with horror, because the man standing over her had no nose! Seeing her reaction, he re-covered his face below his eyes with a handkerchief, and gently asked her why she had been trespassing on his estate. She explained that she had been looking for her dog, upon which Tregeagle, who had been watching his master's treatment of the girl with rising and frustration, suggested shooting the animal, but he dismissed the preposterous suggestion with a wave of the hand.

The gentleman got into conversation with Rosie, asking about her life, what her home was like, and what she usually had to eat. He looked with pity at her ragged clothes and chillblained feet and seemed shocked and saddened when he heard about her life of poverty. The depressing streets and alleyways were her playground, and watery gruel her staple diet. Rosie soon warmed to the funny gentleman and innocently asked why he had no nose, to which he replied that he had been born that way and told her about a girl he had once loved, and how he had been unable to approach her because of his deformed face. He cried unashamedly as he unburdened himself to her. At the end of his story he paced about in front of the fire, wiping the bitter tears from his eyes, then left the room and made his way to the pantry. He returned with a huge bone covered with slivers of meat. He gave it to Chip, but he had never seen a bone like it before, and wore himself out trying to tackle it. Then gazing thoughtfully into the blazing log fire, the man suddenly said, "Rosie, I will give you somewhere to play."

Later in the evening he gave her a small canvas bag full of guineas, then ordered Mr Tregeagle to escort her safely back home. In the bag was a brief sad note, disclosing that he was dying of a wasting disease, and wasn't expected to see the New Year, which proved to be true. On Christmas Day, a funeral hearse was seen trundling into the estate, pulled by a team of gleaming black horses, with large ostrich-feather plumes tossing on their heads.

In the May of the following year, the Grange and its adjoining properties were demolished, and the estate was levelled and grassed over, leaving no trace of the old mansion. A park was built on the land – a park which was named Wavertree Playground. Liverpool City Council was presented with this park in the owner's will, with the stipulation that he was to remain anonymous. He left specific instructions: 'The park is to be a place for the poor children to run and play in.'

Twelve thousand children were invited to the opening ceremony, and each of them was given free milk and cakes. The exciting day culminated in a grand firework display. One of the twelve thousand children was Rosie Sparks, and while all the other children were dashing about enjoying the novelty of the wide open spaces, she thought about the man with the disfigured face, and quietly whispered to herself a grateful thankyou.

Today, in Liverpool, children still play in the park that was donated to them by the mysterious man from the Grange. Because the magnanimous gentleman's identity was never discovered, the local residents aptly called the park 'The Mystery'. Rosie Sparks grew up and had children of her own, and one of them was Molly, the woman who related the tale to me.

THE CAVEMAN OF VICTORIA PARK

In 1870, in the Liverpool district of Wavertree, Patrick O'Connor, an iron-monger, lived with his wife at a house on North Drive, Victoria Park. The couple decided to adopt a baby girl who had been born blind and called her Jessica. Her own mother had died in childbirth and the father had callously abandoned the baby because she was blind. The sight of the helpless infant in the orphanage had tugged at Mrs O'Connor's heartstrings. "When I saw Jessica lying there," she recalled, "unable to see and so helpless, I just knew I had to have her."

By the time Jessica was six, in 1876, Mrs O'Connor had borne her husband a baby boy, William, and Jessica's life revolved around her cute little baby brother. Despite her disability, she was allowed to push his huge hooded pram around the back garden of the house on North Drive. Mrs O'Connor would supervise her most of the time, but not on one particular afternoon, when something terrible happened. Two boys climbed on top of the garden wall and one of them shouted, "Hah! Look! There's that stupid blind girl."

The other boy sneered and said, "Yeah, she talks to herself as well. She must be mad."

They started laughing and wolf-whistling and one of them threw a clod of dry earth, which hit Jessica on the forehead. She ran towards the house, crying hysterically, with tears and mud mingling on her face and the insensitive boys scarpered. Mrs O'Connor found Jessica curled up under the kitchen table.

That night, Mr O'Connor sat Jessica on his knee before bedtime. "Are you going to say your prayers, Jess?" he asked.

The girl nodded, saying, "I have to thank Jesus for lots of things."

Mr O'Connor, knowing about the incident with the two boys, hugged her and said, "Really, pet?"

He took the child to her bedroom and watched her kneel at the bottom of her bed, where she earnestly recited the Lord's Prayer, then added her own, more personal prayers: "Thank you, Lord, for the sun that I love feeling on my face, and when the dragonflies hum. Thank you for the nice smells of the flowers in the garden. And thank you for the sound of my baby brother when he laughs. I love him and have told him about you ..."

Tears rolled down Mr O'Connor's face; he felt so humbled by this child who never complained about her disability, and was so thankful for all the things that most people took for granted. Then he heard her whisper something which intrigued him, "... and thank you for my secret friend,"

Mr O'Connor told his wife about Jessica's mysterious friend and was surprised to find that she already knew.

"She's told me all about him. He's a caveman. Well, from her descriptions he is. She says he's a huge man with long hair who wears animal furs. ... oh, and he carries a big axe!"

"She must have overheard someone talking about cavemen. She's got a good imagination, God bless her."

Autumn arrived, and Mr O'Connor collected all the fallen leaves and burnt them at the end of the garden. That night, his wife was in the kitchen, when she happened to look out of the window. She saw the smouldering embers and then noticed the shadow of a strange-looking man crouched down by the side of them. His unkempt hair was very long, and he had a straggly beard which reached nearly down to his navel. His arms were grubby and bare, as was his chest.

She ran up the four flights of stairs to wake her husband, who had decided to have an early night. Patrick O'Connor ran downstairs with a shotgun and peeped out of the kitchen window, but could see nothing but the smouldering leaves. Mrs O'Connor insisted on what she had seen, and gave a full description, but he just shrugged his shoulders, bolted the door, and went back to bed, yawning and shaking his head.

A few days later, Jessica came into the house wearing a strange primitive bracelet. It was made from small pieces of sharp stone of different colours, one of which Mr O'Connor recognised as flint. When they asked who had given her the bracelet, she hung her head sheepishly, eventually admitting it was the caveman. This made the O'Connors feel decidedly uneasy. Who was this strange friend of hers? Was he a figment of her imagination? Or did he really exist? After all, Mrs O'Connor had seen someone in the garden who looked like a caveman – and she wasn't given to flights of fancy.

Shortly afterwards, an elderly neighbour reported seeing the ghostly caveman in broad daylight, wandering about the O'Connors' garden. She claimed that he was wearing animal furs and had leathery strips of animal skin wrapped around his legs and feet. He also carried what seemed to be a crude axe. One moment he had been there, the next he was gone.

Mr O'Connor was finally convinced when he heard a commotion on North Drive. The two boys who had tormented Jessica came running into the O'Connors' shop on the High Street, saying that a mad tramp had attacked them, and was now in Mr O'Connor's garden. Patrick went to investigate, and sure enough, at the end of the garden, was the fabled caveman, stooping down over Jessica with a smile on his face. "What's your game?" O'Connor shouted, and the ghost backed away as he approached and melted into the garden wall.

From that day on, Mr O'Connor was a convert, who was openly prepared to admit that there were such things as ghosts. He even told a friend who had built their house about the ghost, and the builder told him that in 1867, during the construction of the houses on North Drive, workmen uncovered a number of Bronze Age burial urns, dating from before 1000 BC, containing human remains and flint arrowheads.

Worried about his daughter's safety, Mr O'Connor begged the local priest to bless the garden, and the apparition of the caveman was seen no more.

Also, on a happy note, three years later, little Jessica was struck down with whooping cough. She survived, and as a side effect, regained her sight. The first thing she saw was her little brother's smiling face.

INDIA RUBBER MENACE

In 1949, a cargo of India rubber arrived at Liverpool Docks. In the hold of the same ship, were several crates of African artifacts, including shrunken heads, tribal spears and shields and several elaborately carved wooden masks, which were used by the witchdoctors of a Nigerian tribe. These items were destined to be exhibited at the Liverpool Museum in William Brown Street.

During the unloading of the artifacts, a crate slipped from the winch cables, and crashed down on to the quayside, spilling its exotic contents. The dockers quickly collected as many items as they could stuff into their pockets. One light-fingered docker named Georgie, decided to keep one of the wooden masks, as he thought it would make a nice talking point on his parlour wall. Two others each pilfered a shrunken head, thinking no one would notice, as there were about twenty of them in the crate.

All three dockers suffered amazing bad luck later that day. During the lunch break, one of them, a man named Brian, was playing a game of poker in a hut on the waterfront, and was winning every game until he had amassed about fifty pounds – a very substantial sum in 1949. When the lunchbreak ended, the dockers left the hut, and just as Brian was gloating over his win, a sudden gust of gale force wind whipped up out of nowhere, battering the quayside and slamming open the hut door, sending ten shilling notes fluttering out across the waterfront like confetti. Dockers scrambled to grab the notes, but every last one of them blew into the River Mersey. Next thing, the mysterious wind died down and it became calm again. In a blind rage at having watched his winnings disappear, Brian took the shrunken head out of his jacket and wondered if it might be cursed.

About an hour later, Alan, the other docker who had taken one of the heads, also experienced a terrible piece of bad luck. Alan wore an eyepatch because having lost his right eye during the war when a piece of shrapnel from a bomb exploding at the docks, damaging it beyond repair. Alan walked into a warehouse where the two young sons of one of the dockers were playing darts. The dartboard was mounted on a door. He opened that door just as one of the lads threw a dart – and it shot straight through the pupil of his good eye. He collapsed from the trauma. Luckily, he was later treated by a highly skilled Rodney Street surgeon, and his remaining eye was saved, but it was never the same again after that freak accident.

That same day, in the late afternoon, a large pallet, measuring about twenty-five feet square, was loaded with several huge, trussed-up blocks of India rubber. The crane operator was transporting the rubber from the ship on to the quayside – when, for reasons that have never been properly explained, the four chains linked to the pallet snapped simultaneously. The huge block of India rubber plummeted sixty feet, and the dockers below yelled out to one another and fanned out from the pallet, like ripples on a lake. Everyone scattered – everyone except Georgie, the one who had stolen the African mask. He looked up as the block of rubber raced towards him. He ran as fast as his legs could carry him and just managed to leap clear in time. The huge bale smashed into the quayside – and then bounced back high into the air!

Now, India rubber is very elastic. Some of the older readers may remember a thing called the 'superball' from the 1970s: a small ball of India rubber, which, when hurled at the ground, would rebound as high as a house and continue bouncing for quite some time.

So Georgie ran down the quayside with the bale of India rubber bouncing crazily after him, almost as if it had a mind of its own and was in deliberate pursuit. Wherever the terrified docker ran, the gigantic block of rubber followed. He ran across a road, and the rubber went that way too, bouncing twenty-five feet into the air after him. It landed on a horse-drawn cart at one point, completely flattening the vehicle and injuring the unfortunate horse into the bargain. Georgie ran back across the road and the bouncing block followed him. In the end, the exhausted and terrified docker dived into the Huskisson Branch Dock to get away from the bouncing bale, and it bounced straight in after him! He tried to resurface but the rubber bale blocked his way and he had to swim out from under it.

Georgie was later treated at the Northern Hospital for shock. He told his friends to remove the mask from his locker and to take it to the museum. When he was being pursued by the block of Indian rubber, weird laughter had convinced him that a malevolent African spirit was deliberately guiding it towards him!

FRANCESCA

On the foggy Sunday evening of 18 December 1904, forty-five-year-old Mary Eccles of Mill Lane rushed into the Police Station on Wavertree High Street and told the station sergeant James Anderson, that her eleven-year-old daughter Lucy had gone missing again. "Oh no! Not again! You shouldn't let her out of your sight, Mrs Eccles, you know what she's like," said Sergeant Anderson.

Anderson's superior, Inspector John Crompton, ordered him to go and look in all the usual places for the wayward girl. With a disgruntled sigh, he gulped down his mug of cocoa, donned his helmet and cape and set out into the cold fog to search for Lucy Eccles, or the 'Wild Child of Wavertree' as she was known at the station.

Ever since Lucy's father had passed away two years before, her behaviour had steadily worsened. Just a few days ago she had gone missing and been found in the highest reaches of a tree in the grounds of Sandown Hall. On a previous occasion, during the summer, outraged anglers had reported the girl to the police after she had stripped naked to take a dip in Wavertree Fish Pond!

On this fog-enshrouded December night, the grumbling sergeant searched orchards, parks, a deserted cottage on

Olive Lane and many more of the uncontrollable girl's usual haunts, but Lucy was nowhere to be found. Just when the policeman was about to give up the search, he saw her emerging from the jade green fog in Wavertree Nook Road, carrying a small, under-nourished mongrel dog.

"Mr Anderson, I found a dog. Look!" she cried excitedly.

Sergeant Anderson shook his head – she seemed to have no understanding of the trouble she caused her family and the police. He scolded her for wandering off, knowing full well that anything he said would go in one ear and out the other, and returned her to her mother on Mill Lane. Knowing that Lucy would throw an appalling tantrum if she tried to make her abandon the dog, Mrs Eccles reluctantly allowed her to keep the scruffy little animal, which she called Luke. Her gallivanting continued and Luke would trail after her for miles around Liverpool, getting into all kinds of mischief with his new playmate.

One summer evening in 1905, the pair were exploring the neighbourhood of Fairfield, when Lucy found a jointed porcelain doll among a pile of refuse in the courtyard of a house. She took an instant liking to the doll, but Luke seemed to regard it with great suspicion. When Mrs Eccles saw the doll, she asked Lucy if she had given her a name. "Just Dolly I suppose, Ma," she said with a shrug.

That evening there was a loud yelp from upstairs and Luke came bounding down and dived under a chair, cowering with fear. Lucy quickly followed, exclaiming, "Ma! That doll's alive! It said its name's Francesca, and it dances too!"

Mrs Eccles just smiled, without bothering to look up from the sock she was darning. She was used to her daughter's tall tales and usually ignored them. Lucy jumped up and down in frustration, angrily yelling, "It's alive, Ma. It's alive!"

She took her mother by the hand and dragged her upstairs, but Francesca was lying limp and lifeless on the bed. Lucy grabbed the doll and shook it, shouting, "Speak! Please speak again!" but the doll remained silent and still. Lucy kept insisting that it could speak and dance, but her mother just sighed, saying, "I believe you, dear," then left the room wondering why she had been blessed with such a difficult daughter.

That night, Mrs Eccles heard Lucy singing in her bedroom, and another voice was singing along with her. The words of the song were, "Alouette, gentille Alouette, Alouette je te plumerai." More than a little surprised, she left her bed and stood outside her daughter's room listening to the two voices, then bent down and peeped through the keyhole. The doll was dancing up and down on the end of the bed! She barged into the room and instantly the doll fell down off the bed and lay motionless on the floor.

While Lucy was at school the next day, Mrs Eccles visited a priest and told him about the dancing doll. He visited the house, and recognised it at once. It had belonged to a child of two of his well-to-do parishioners in Fairfield, who had lost their daughter, Lily, after she had succumbed to a long illness. He had attended her throughout, and knew that her doll had indeed been called Francesca, and that her favourite song had been 'Alouette'.

Mrs Eccles felt ill at ease when she heard all this, but the priest advised her to keep the apparently haunted doll, saying that Lily had been a lovely child, gentle and sweet, who had borne her suffering with patience and serenity. Maybe the doll would be a positive influence on Lucy.

So the doll was returned to Lucy and strangely enough, her unruly behaviour gradually lessened, she settled down and even began to excel at school.

MONKEY SNATCH

Mr William Judcote, a seventy-year-old property tycoon from Liverpool, sat in his high-backed wicker chair admiring the colourful flowery acres of his garden. The date was 9 July 1870 – a perfect summer's day. Behind him stood his white cottage with its picturesque thatched roof – his country retreat in the pretty Somerset village of Manxbridge. He was sipping a measure of fine whisky, as he watched his exotic pet, Hulch, climbing a sycamore tree. Hulch was a powerful, muscular monkey who measured over five feet in height when he stood on his hind legs. Judcote had found him on the loose in Liverpool, but had never discovered how he had come to be in the port. There was some speculation that he had been brought in through the docks by a sailor and then abandoned when he grew too large. The most arresting thing about Hulch was his almost human eyes. Most primates have brown eyes, but he had highly expressive eyes of a deep azure blue.

Anyway, on this day, the monkey swung down from the tree and watched his master in fascination as he drank the whisky. Mr Judcote laughed and poured a shot for him in a small porcelain teacup. The animal sniffed it, put it to his lips, then threw back his head and drank it down in one go. He then clutched his throat and rolled about comically across the lawn. Mr Judcote laughed at Hulch's antics, as he loped off to chase a rabbit it had spotted at the bottom of the garden.

On the adjoining plot of land there was a smaller cottage, built by Mr Judcote for his former Liverpudlian maid, Mrs Hemmingway, and her family. She had been recently widowed and was doing a very good job of rearing her seven-year-old son, her six-year-old daughter Clara and her nine-month-old baby, Lizzie, who had been born on Duke Street and recently brought to Manxbridge.

On this hot July day, Clara was allowed to look after baby Lizzie, and she had dressed her in a pink, petal-rimmed bonnet and a little peach-coloured dress. She then walked into the garden, rocking the baby in her arms. From a tree across the field, Hulch watched Clara holding the infant, and out of curiosity perhaps, he nimbly scrambled down the tree and loped over to them to get a closer look. Clara waved her finger at him and told him he wasn't allowed in the garden. Hulch took no notice and tried to snatch at the baby's dress. Clara ran inside shouting for her mother, but she had popped out to the shops in the local village. Clara slammed the door in the monkey's face, but he kept looking through the windows with an expression of utmost concern, which seemed to be directed at the baby. Clara and her brother laughed at his comical face pressed against the window, but this was where events took a nasty turn.

About ten minutes later, Clara's older brother came out of the house with one of her dolls, which he had deliberately dressed in the baby's clothes. He then ran outside, and threw the doll up in the air, laughing as he caught it, knowing that poor old Hulch would be tricked into thinking it was Lizzie. The monkey came screaming out of a hedge and the lad ran back inside, clutching the doll. He closed the door, and he and Clara fell about laughing as the monkey's frantic face peered in turn through each window.

Then their mother returned and as she entered the cottage with her basket of groceries, Hulch barged past her, knocking it out of her hand. He seized Lizzie from her cot, and ran back outside as Clara and her mother screamed. He ran across a field of barley with the stunned baby cradled in his great, hairy arms. When William Judcote was informed, he summoned his seven servants, and they boarded two carriages to the village, while Judcote mounted his horse and rode like the devil after the baby-snatching monkey.

When he reached Manxbridge, he found the place in turmoil, with people running about excitedly. Then he saw, to his horror, that Hulch was crawling over the rooftops, still cradling Lizzie, who appeared to be more bemused than afraid. The villagers took up the chase wielding pitchforks, sticks and even blunderbusses. One man fell and broke his legs as he tried to intercept the monkey on a roof. Hearts missed a beat as Hulch leapt across a wide gap between two roofs. Then they lost sight of him. People tried to comfort Mrs Hemmingway, but she was hysterical, and severely scolded her children when a servant told her that he had seen them taunting the monkey.

Not long afterwards, Hulch appeared by a large chimney stack above the village inn – his long arms empty! Mrs Hemmingway fainted, as Hulch gibbered and gazed incomprehendingly at the sea of faces below – faces now filled with hatred. Three villagers aimed their blunderbusses and an old flintlock at him and fired a volley. Hulch fell backwards and toppled down the far side of the roof.

When the crowds surged round the back of the inn, they found a trail of blood, which led down a short dusty lane to a barn, where bales of hay and wool were stored. Inside the barn, near the door, the wounded animal lay prostrate, quivering with shock, with a gunshot wound in his shoulder. He was crawling agonisingly slowly across the floor towards the bales of hay, when a villager aimed a blunderbuss directly at him. Mr Judcote stood in his way, begging him to hold fire. A heated argument ensued, but then everyone fell silent when they heard the sounds of a baby crying.

Over the stack of hay was baby Lizzie, lying on a bale of wool and holding a large rosy apple. She was completely unharmed. Mr Judcote had Hulch taken back to his cottage, where he paid a physician to treat him, and he managed to save his life. Taking into consideration the fact that the monkey had thought he was rescuing Lizzie from harm on the day he snatched her, his life was spared, and he later became Lizzie's pet as she grew up.

The life expectancy of a chimpanzee is fifty years. Hulch lived for another eighteen, but eventually became very grey and arthritic. He was allowed into the village church on the day that Lizzie Hemingway was married and shortly afterwards, he went quietly off to the woods to die.

KILLED BY A DEAD MAN

In 1872, Henry Taylor, a sixty-six-year-old confidence trickster from Winsford in Cheshire, embezzled and swindled his way across England. He impersonated a policeman in Liverpool, and wormed his way into an old woman's house and conned her out of her life savings by telling her that he would put the money in a safe at the police station. Of course, the money was never seen again. Then the despicable Mr Taylor set up a bogus collection for the blind at Telford, before quickly vacating that town. He then turned up in Wolverhampton, claiming he could cure any ailment by using his hypnotic powers, but he made the mistake of trying deceive the wife of a police sergeant with his latest scam, and narrowly escaped arrest.

Taylor subsequently fled to London, where he invented a new alias, this time introducing himself as Arthur Sexton. He moved into a lodging house in the Paddington area, and ingratiated himself with the landlady, Mrs Williams, originally from Liverpool, who was looking after her sick seventy-five-year-old husband Archie. Archie Williams took an instant dislike to the new lodger, and warned his wife there was something evil about him. Mrs Williams felt that her husband had become isolated and grumpy because of his illness, and assured him that the new lodger was a charming man with impeccable manners.

However, she was soon to see Taylor in his true colours – literally – when he stripped off all his clothes one night and confronted her in the kitchen, declaring that he wanted to make love to her. She screamed and warned him to leave her alone, or she would call the police. Taylor skulked off but returned unabashed, this time partly clothed, and begged Mrs Williams to let him stay. He explained that her beauty had overwhelmed him and made him act like a love-struck fool. He even managed to produce real tears as he knelt before the gullible woman, clutching at her apron and sobbing pitifully.

He must have given a very convincing performance, because she did forgive him, and that night they talked until midnight, and she told him about her nagging worry that if her husband should die, she would be terribly lonely. Very unwisely, she also disclosed that she stood to receive a substantial insurance payout, adding that it could never replace her dear husband Archie.

By a strange twist of fate, Archie did pass away that night as he slept beside his wife. After the tragedy – or stroke of good luck – as Henry Taylor saw it, he stuck to the landlady like glue as he schemed up ways to relieve her of the insurance money. Wearing a long face, he attended the funeral service, then accompanied her to the place of burial, which was London's Kensal Green cemetery.

Six pallbearers carefully manoevred the heavy lead-lined coffin from the rain-lashed hearse and proceeded slowly down the path, when suddenly, it became apparent that the front pallbearer was the worse for drink. Horrified, the chief pallbearer ordered the man to the back of the coffin, and as he attempted to obey this command, he slipped in the mud, and the rain-drenched coffin started to slide. Mrs Williams screamed and Henry Taylor rushed forward to try and get a grip of the heavy coffin, but he too slipped in the mud and fell on to his back. The end of the coffin crashed down on him, smashing straight into his Adam's apple and driving his bottom jaw up through the roof of his mouth.

Slithering about in the mud, the pallbearers struggled to wrench the heavy oak coffin off Henry Taylor. As they did so, he instinctively put his hand to his face and pulled his shattered jaw apart, causing a communal shudder to pass through all the mourners.

He was taken to hospital, but died minutes after arrival from traumatic shock. At the morgue, the police established his identity from various documents in his jacket, realising that the dead man was the callous confidence trickster who was wanted by police forces across the country. All sympathy for the victim of the freak accident evaporated, and the detectives agreed that it was a case of poetic justice and that Mrs Williams had had a very narrow escape.

THE SAD TALE OF MADGE KIRBY

In the back yard of a certain house on Underley Street, in the Edge Hill area of Liverpool, there is a dark stubborn stain which is said to be the ingrained trace of a murdered child's blood. Many years ago, when my sister lived in this street, I was shown the stain. It is a dark, disc-shaped discolouration on the back step, about four inches in diameter. Local legend has it that it is the blood of Madge Kirby, an Edwardian child who was abducted and killed.

I first heard of the sad tale of Madge from my grandmother, Rose Slemen, when I was a child. I fondly recall the stormy afternoon I played truant and was collared by my grandmother, skipping up Crown Street. She told me that I could have been snatched by a stranger, and I, being morbidly curious, went to her home in Myrtle Gardens, eagerly asking what might have happened to me had I been picked up by a stranger. When I reached my gran's home, she told me the following true story.

It all began at 4.30pm on the dark wintry afternoon of Monday, 6 January 1908. Seven-year-old Margaret Kirby, known affectionately as Madge, was playing near the reservoir in Farnworth Street, Kensington, just around the corner from her home at Number 55 Romily Street. Her father David was a plumber, but work had been slow because of his severe depression, brought on by the loss of his wife, who had died from a long illness, just a fortnight before, during the Christmas period.

On that cold afternoon in 1908, as twilight gathered, a man in dark clothes approached Madge, who was playing in the street with her best friend Annie McGovern. "Would you like to go with me for some sweets?" he asked in a soft well-spoken voice. He had probably chosen Madge because she stood out amongst her peers because of her beauty. She nodded, and innocently took his hand and walked away with him into the wintry murk. When Madge did not return home for her tea, her father went in search of her, without success. He listened with dread when Annie and several other children told him about the man who had lured her away with the promise of sweets – the classic approach of the paedophile.

The police lost no time in launching a wide-scale search for the missing girl. Lakes were dragged, parks scoured, over five thousand empty houses were searched and there were door-to-door enquiries in Kensington and parts of Edge Hill, but Madge could not be found. David Kirby was devastated by his daughter's abduction and his sisters and three-year-old son could only provide only a modicum of consolation for him. The police asked for a detailed description of his missing daughter, to be circulated to police stations throughout Lancashire. Fighting back hot tears, David told them that Madge had been wearing a black shirt with worn sleeves, a blue pinafore, a black velvet bonnet with black strings, black stockings and laced boots. He broke down completely as he described his beloved daughter's brown hair, sky-blue eyes and very fair, fresh-faced complexion.

In St Michael's School, which Madge Kirby had attended, the teachers and children said a prayer each day for her safe return. The months wore on, but still no trace of Madge could be found – until eight months later, on the morning of Tuesday, 21 August, when a man going to work came upon a dirty old onion sack, outside a condemned house on Great Newton Street, off London Road. That sack contained the remains of a scantily-clad girl. The body of Madge Kirby had been found at last. Now the hunt was on for her killer.

The police lost no time in launching a murder hunt, but their investigations were hampered by the public, large numbers of whom congregated outside the Prescot Street police station, waiting for any new developments in the case. Detectives noted the onion sack was dry, yet the pavement was wet from a recent rainfall and determined that it had been kept in the cellar of the derelict house.

On the night after the body was found, two policemen rushed out of the police station with a bloodhound leading the way. The dog led them in a westerly direction and the great mob followed. Six of them raced after the police on bicycles, two elderly men were pushed along in their wheelchairs and several women pushed prams as they joined the hunt. Over two thousand people poured down Prescot Street, many of them carrying refreshments, towards the city centre, but little did they know that the bloodhound they were following, impressive though it was, was but a decoy.

Shortly after midnight, one of the most sensitive bloodhounds ever deployed by the Lancashire Constabulary emerged from the police station and immediately took up the faded but still useable scent he had taken from the murdered child's clothes. The dog's name was Czar, and he had been loaned from a dog-handler named Pakenham. Czar took the police on a curious meandering trail that wound through the Botanic Gardens, then on to a strip of secluded waste ground on the eastern extremities of Edge Lane. From there, he led them to Tunnel Road and on to Edge Hill railway station. In an unusually excited state, Czar dragged the policeman to the city centre-bound platform and stood stock still, gazing at the tunnel. He convulsed and sniffed the air. That tunnel led to Lime Street.

Czar was bundled into a cab, and the taxi driver was instructed to go to Lime Street station, where the bloodhound bolted straight for platform one. He barked and howled at the tunnel, which the dog's owner took to mean that Madge Kirby's killer had left Liverpool for the Midlands, as trains from that platform were bound for Birmingham. There, the tantalising trail went cold.

Police received a letter, purportedly from the child killer, which stated that he had once lived as a lodger on the premises where the body was found, and that he had kept the key and so had access to the empty house. He said he had taken Madge there and sadistically killed her. Eight months later he had decided to 'let the world know' what had become of Madge Kirby, so he dragged her badly-decomposed remains from the cellar and placed them in the onion sack, which was then left on the pavement. The mystery deepened when several people came forward and told police that they had spotted a sinister individual, dressed as a woman, climbing over the back yard wall of the empty house on Great Newton Street on the morning of the body's discovery. Police later suspected a man named Thompson who had lodged in Great Newton Street, but they were never able to track him down.

Madge's heartbroken father never recovered from the murder, and died weeks after his beloved daughter's body was found. Today, Madge Kirby lies at rest in Ford cemetery, the forgotten victim of an Edwardian child-killer. Which grave in Liverpool, or perhaps Birmingham, contains the remains of Madge Kirby's murderer? A rumour persisted that the killer lived on Underley Street, and that he had been responsible for several attacks on children and young women in the alleyways off Smithdown Road in 1907, months before the Madge Kirby outrage. Some said he was a sailor, others that he had the appearance of a clerk.

Perhaps the psychopathic paedophile worked at Edge Hill railway station, which would account for Czar's erratic behaviour at the Edge Hill and Lime Street tunnels. Perhaps he had not fled to another city after all, but worked on those railway lines. He only had to take the child through the gaslit streets of Kensington via a direct route to the murder scene – from Edge Hill station to Lime Street, then walk the short distance to Great Newton Street.

The killer cheated the hangman, and now lies mouldering in his grave, but perhaps his troubled, remorse-filled spirit still wanders the night, revisiting the scenes of his heinous crimes. Over the years, a shadowy man in black has been seen walking silently up Romily Street and Jubilee Drive with his head bowed. The consensus of the older folks residing in the area of the haunting in the 1950s was that the dark apparition was the restless earthbound shade of Madge Kirby's killer, retracing each step of his prowling itinerary of long ago, whilst dreading the arrival of the Highest Judge of all, on Judgement Day ...

LOVING MEMORY

One snowy January afternoon in 1877, shopkeeper Alfred
Roddy locked up his Dale Street shop earlier than usual – at
about four o'clock – and began the walk home to his house
near to where the Churchill Way Flyover is now situated,
close to Crosshall Street. Mr Roddy, who was just the right
side of seventy, was a widower who had something of a
lonely existence. He had lived on his own since the death of
his wife ten years before, and even though he had been very
fond of her when she was alive, he had only truly loved one
woman in his life, when he was forty.

The one whom he had loved but lost, was a poor girl
from Everton called Hannah Cordwainer. She had been
only eighteen but he had fallen passionately in love with
her from the moment he had set eyes upon her, and she
had regarded him in the same way. Unfortunately, Hannah
was very impoverished and Alfred Roddy's father had
pressured him into marrying a woman nearer to his own
age – Agnes Black, the daughter of a rich businessman. To
make matters worse, Hannah's Catholic father had
threatened to disown her if she married a Protestant such
as Alfred Roddy. Hannah was forbidden to go near him and
Alfred's father and her parents forced him to give up his
love for her.

Now, at the age of sixty-nine, Alfred realised just how
much love he felt for Hannah, because in most people, the
passage of time quickly dilutes such feelings, but Alfred
Roddy still dreamt of Hannah Cordwainer, and when he
drank his whisky nightcap at midnight, he tortured himself
with thoughts of what might have been.

On this wintry afternoon, he was lost in such thoughts

when he was knocked down on the frosted cobbled road by a wagon. The horse had bolted and as the driver struggled to regain control, people rushed to his aid. He was taken home, where a doctor treated him for minor cuts and bruises, but during the fall he had hit his head on the cobbles, and the concussion had left him with severe amnesia. He didn't even know his own name. A neighbour offered to look after him at his home, as he didn't have any relatives she knew of, and the doctor said he would call each day to ascertain the severity of the head injury.

Alfred Roddy was put to bed, and his neighbour Mrs Campbell kindly looked after him. His amnesia showed no signs of lifting after a week, and Mrs Campbell became very weary, because she also had her own family to look after. One day she asked the friend of a cousin to help out, and the woman duly arrived at the house. This helper was a pretty woman in her forties and Alfred Roddy became very animated when he saw her. He told her she had beautiful eyes, and suddenly, the woman gasped. Turning to Mrs Campbell, she asked if he was Alfred Roddy. When the answer came in the affirmative, the woman, who, yes, was Hannah Cordwainer, whispered that she had once been in love with him, almost thirty years before. Hannah sat on Alfred's bed and he held her hand. "I don't know who you are, and yet I love you," he said. "Did I once know you?"

As soon as Hannah revealed her name, Alfred began to study her in total astonishment, and tears started to fall from his eyes. "Why do I cry?" he asked. "You must have been close to my heart. Are you my wife?"

Hannah became tearful too, and she kissed Alfred, who suddenly muttered one word – Hannah. The fog of amnesia had blotted out virtually all of Alfred Roddy's life, but it had been unable to erase his cherished memories of Hannah.

Gradually, Alfred's memory returned and he and Hannah fell in love all over again. They were married that July.

THE DANCING DRESS

On the Wednesday night of 12 April 1978, Graham, from Crosby, was in a Liverpool pub in Williamson Square, celebrating Liverpool's three nil victory over Borussia Moenchengladbach. During the celebrations, Graham noticed an attractive red-head, sitting at the bar with some friends. Being slightly intoxicated and so full of Dutch courage, he edged over to the woman and asked if he could buy her a drink. She politely replied, "No thanks," and continued her conversation. The last orders bell was rung, and over the clamour and hubbub of the drinkers, the barman called, "Come on now, drink up".

Graham ignored the rebuff because she was the most beautiful woman he had seen in years, and felt compelled to let her know his feelings. He overheard her saying to her friends that she would be there on Saturday, before going on to Mr Pickwick's nightclub. Graham went home that night to Crosby, and on Saturday evening he was so eager to see her again, that he persuaded a friend to drive him to Liverpool, where he was dropped off in Dawson Street, close to Williamson Square. He walked over to the pub where he had met the woman of his dreams and pushed open the door. His eyes quickly scanned the line of drinkers and his heart skipped a beat when he saw her sitting on a bar-stool. She looked sensational in a low cut top with her hair swept up in an elegant knot. Graham edged towards her, and saw that she was finishing off a glass of Baileys, so he ordered another, and placed it in front of her saying, "You look absolutely beautiful."

She smiled and whispered "Thanks" and as she sipped the Baileys they started to talk. Her name was Cathy and she had just come out of a relationship and was in no hurry to begin another one. Graham said he was also single, and had finished a long-term relationship a while back. He had been with Philomena for seven years, but she had left him for someone else exactly a year ago, in April. They seemed to get on well and he ended up taking his beautiful new acquaintance to the Silver Sands club.

At about one o'clock, the DJ put on a slow record, but instead of taking Cathy in his arms and dancing with her, Graham became very nervous. The song on the turntable was 'Chanson d'Amour' by The Manhattan Transfer. The song had been a number one hit a year ago and was originally recorded in 1961. Cathy noticed his strange reaction immediately the song was played. With a look of dread in his eyes, he pulled her out of the club and on to the cold and windy street. She protested that she had left her coat in the club, but Graham prevented her from going back inside. He said he knew the club's owner and promised to collect her coat in the morning. When Cathy persisted in trying to return to the nightclub, he hailed a taxi, and almost bundled her into the vehicle. The cab took them to Graham's home on Winchester Avenue in Crosby. Cathy kept asking him why he had left the club in such a hurry, and he seemed stuck for an answer. Despite having some misgivings about his behaviour, she was strongly attracted to Graham and that night they slept together, and later started going steady.

The relationship progressed, and one Saturday morning, at around three o'clock, she was lying next to him in bed.

They had just returned from a night out and Cathy had flung her new scarlet dress over a chair in the bedroom and fallen into bed exhausted. Graham was asleep in seconds, but once in bed, Cathy suddenly felt wide awake and lit up a cigarette. She reached over to the clock radio and switched it on, but turned off the bedside lamp, because there was enough light coming into the room from outside. She carefully lowered the volume so as not to wake Graham and then adjusted the tuner, searching for something relaxing. The faint strains of a melody came drifting in on Radio Luxembourg – 'Chanson d'Amour'.

As the song played, Cathy detected a rich, sweet-scented aroma in the air. A few moments later, her discarded dress rose up off the chair, as if some invisible figure was inside it. The gaudy garment danced in time to the music, and waltzed across the bedroom. She let out a scream that not only sent Graham flying out of bed, but brought the next-door neighbours hurrying to his front door. He grabbed the radio and switched it off, then clicked on the bedside lamp. Where was Cathy? He found her downstairs in a terrible state, wearing one of his shirts. She told him to fetch a pair of jeans, as she was certainly never going to wear the red dress again. He tried to calm her, but Cathy was very badly shaken and refused to go back to bed, demanding that Graham take her home.

"This is your home isn't it?"

"Not any more," said Cathy, and she warned him that she would order herself a cab if he refused to drive her. Graham pointed out that he couldn't legally drive, as he had been drinking at the club, so Cathy telephoned her brother-in-law, who came to pick her up. Graham begged her to stay, but she flatly refused – she was terrified of anything to do with the world of the supernatural and the dancing dress was just too much for her. Her intuition told her that somehow Graham had something to do with the ghostly goings-on, at which he seemed stuck for words. After that night Cathy stopped seeing him.

Graham died in 1980, and Cathy later heard a strange rumour. In 1977, before he met her, Graham was due to marry his long-term girlfriend, when she was diagnosed with breast cancer and she died before the wedding date. 'Chanson d'Amour' had been her favourite song and was to have been played at the wedding. On her deathbed Graham had promised never to love another. Nevertheless, just months after her death, Graham was holding hands with a new girlfriend across a table in a bistro, when an instrumental version of 'Chanson d'Amour' came over the loudspeakers. Suddenly, the glass containing his drink shattered, spraying them both with wine and razor-sharp shards of glass. From that time onwards, the girl's spirit was conjured up every time he heard her favourite song, which explains the mystery of the dancing dress.

POLLY

In Liverpool's Rodney Street, there is a very old dwelling that was once a nursing home and which closed its doors for good a few years ago. Around the mid-1970s, a spate of ghostly activity broke out at the home, and one of the first people to witness these was the matron, but she chose to say nothing at first, for fear of alarming the staff and patients.

However, a young nurse called Brenda was working on the nightshift one January evening at eleven o'clock, when she heard the sounds of what seemed to be a woman sobbing somewhere in the upper floors of the house. At first, she thought it was a patient, but then she heard the dull footfall of someone coming down the stairs. Waiting in suspense at the foot of the stairs, Brenda saw the crying woman reach the second floor landing and turn to face her as she came down the stairs. She was dressed in a long white featureless garment like an old-fashioned nightgown and was aged between twenty and twenty-five years of age. Brenda's heart pounded, because she was partially transparent, and not only was her face as pale as chalk, but two dark gashes scarred her wrists and blood was flowing copiously from them. The phantom's ethereal cheeks glistened as tears flowed from a pair of large black sorrowful eyes. The 'night-gown' was almost certainly a burial shroud.

Filled with a rising sensation of terror, Brenda fled down the stairs, unable to cry out. The ghost shadowed her and Brenda dashed into the dark empty office that was occupied by the matron during the day. She was so petrified that she slammed the door shut and cowered under the desk, as the sobbing got nearer and nearer. The ghost passed straight through the closed door and glided towards the desk. The apparition was so vivid that Brenda could clearly see its bare ashen feet standing by the desk. She screwed her eyes tightly shut and fervently made the sign of the cross and when she opened them, the ghost had gone. When she was sure that it was safe to come out, she switched on every light in the building and alerted two other nurses. The three of them on duty that night were so agitated, they even refused to go to the toilet alone.

The next day, Brenda told the matron about her experience. To her surprise, she said that she had also seen the woman in white – exactly three years before, on 9 January. She revealed that she had always been a bit psychic, but had never told anyone of her gift, for fear of ridicule. When she had seen the troubled spectre coming down the stairs, she had received the strong impression that its name was Polly. Matron had also experienced an overpowering feeling of sorrow, which made her throat close up. Seconds afterwards, the wraith had melted away.

Rather than putting her mind at rest, this new information made Brenda feel even more alarmed, because it confirmed her worst fears; the place was haunted and she could be confronted by the ghostly woman at any time. News of the haunting spread through the home and beyond, and one of the cleaners who had worked there in the past said that she had once seen a ghostly nun walking up the same stairs with her back to her. From that day on, Brenda refused to work nights, and even during the day her nerves remained taut while she was on duty.

Around this time, Brenda started dating John David, whose hobby was ghost hunting. He possessed all the equipment for this unusual pastime, and often worked with a medium named Bill Holroyd, an epileptic young man who had quite a reputation for 'empathising' with ghosts. Unlike most mediums, Holroyd refused to be paid for a gift which he claimed had been given to him by "a higher authority". He was fascinated by her encounter with the woman in white, and constantly asked her if he could investigate the case. She checked with matron, who refused his request at first, but later relented, when the ghost continued to make alarming appearances at the home. She allowed John and his mediumistic associate a few hours, on the condition that they kept a low profile, and promised not to talk to anyone from the newspapers. John and Bill gave their word not to seek any media attention.

About a week later, just before midnight, Bill warned the three nurses on duty to stay in their staffroom; the ghost was about to walk, he told them, and he was right. First came the crying sound – then the pale, pathetic figure descended the stairs. John was positioned with a camera loaded with infra red film halfway up the stairs and he clicked on his audio cassette recorder. Bill Holroyd bravely intercepted the ghost, curious to see if it would walk right through him, but instead it halted and gazed at him with a look of indescribable anguish. Bill gently asked her questions about her name and why she was so restless. Almost four minutes elapsed, and during that eternity of heightened suspense, John saw the girl's mouth faintly flicker. Then she slowly faded away, as he reached out slowly to touch the air where she had stood.

The medium came downstairs and imparted all of the information he had received from the ghost. Her name was Mary Burrows, but she had been known as Polly. She had lived nearby in Falkner Square with her sisters and father and had been deeply in love with a poor carpenter named Samuel. She had become pregnant with his child, and her outraged father had had Samuel dragged into a solicitor's office, where he was coerced into signing a contract which stipulated that he would receive a large sum of money if he would stop seeing Polly. Samuel had chosen the money instead of Polly.

Having a child out of wedlock was regarded as scandalous in Victorian times and Polly was locked away in a convent until the birth, after which the nuns gave the baby away to a childless couple. Polly was convinced that Samuel would come and rescue her, but after months of waiting, she realised that he no longer cared for her, and in the emotional crisis which ensued, she slashed her wrists and bled to death.

All of this information was checked and verified. The electoral registers were examined, and it was established that in Victorian times, nuns did indeed run a home for unmarried mothers at the Rodney Street house, which was presently occupied by the nursing home. Further research ascertained that a Burrows family had lived in Falkner Square during that period. The medium spent almost a week at the nursing home, trying his utmost to persuade the tormented spirit of Polly Burrows to go to the world of peaceful spirits where she belonged, but she refused, and as far as I know, Polly still haunts the house on Rodney Street where she took her own life in a moment of intense despair.

THE GHOST OF STRAWBERRY FIELDS

Strawberry Fields, once an orphanage on Beaconsfield Road, in the Woolton district of Liverpool, is familiar across the world, as the subject of a famous Beatles song. The Salvation Army orphanage was founded in 1936 and in the following year a strange incident took place in its vicinity.

In December 1937, seven-year-old Elsie, from Liverpool, lost her mother to cancer. Her father had already died when she was four. The girl was temporarily placed in the care of the Strawberry Fields orphanage just three days before Christmas, until the authorities could find a suitable long term placement for her.

On the dark snowy morning of Christmas Eve, Elsie lay listlessly in bed, overcome with loneliness and grief. She decided to write a letter to Father Christmas, asking him if he could leave her a baby brother. She found a pen and paper and after she had written the note, she folded it and put on her coat and beret. She somehow managed to sneak out of the grounds without being caught, to wander off in search of a post box. She soon found one, and filled with childish optimism, she posted her note. Her intention was to go straight back to Strawberry Fields, but somehow she lost her way.

Elsie trudged through the snow down a lane off Yew Tree Road, where she came upon a cottage. Outside in the garden stood a snowman wearing a top hat. She took a peep through the cottage window and saw a scene which made her heart burn with sorrow and envy. A woman in a long pink dress was surrounded by a circle of laughing young girls and boys, all holding hands as they danced around her. In the background stood a beautifully decorated Christmas tree and green and red garlands and colourful paper decorations festooned the ceilings. The ring of children broke up, and one of them, a little boy with chestnut-coloured hair, looked up at the window and caught sight of Elsie's sad face pressed against the pane. He drew the woman's attention to Elsie's presence, and she quickly went outside to find the child.

Anxious that she was in for a scolding, Elsie tried to conceal herself behind the top-hatted snowman, but the woman soon found her, and leant towards her smiling, "Good morning, dear," she said, warmly. Elsie told her she was lost, so the woman took her inside where she was introduced to the children and given a seat before a cosy hearth. She was invited to join in the children's games, and afterwards sat at a long table and enjoyed a hearty breakfast, followed by Christmas pudding and cake.

Sometime later, a grandfather clock struck eight o'clock as the pale light of morning filtered through the windows. The lady in the pink dress put on a long coat and a large white bonnet decked with flowers, then took Elsie by the hand. She led her out of the cottage as the children frowned and said their goodbyes. Elsie looked back at the end of the path and watched them waving from the windows. She wished she could have stayed with them, as she did not have a friend in the world.

The little orphan was led to the gates of Strawberry Fields, at which point the woman vanished after hugging her. Elsie hurried inside and related her account of the kind lady and the children at the lovely cottage. One of the musicians in the Salvation Army band was intrigued by the yuletide mystery, and went in search of the cottage with Elsie on Christmas Day, but was unable to find it.

In January of the new year, a woman arrived at the orphanage to claim Elsie; an Aunt Julia she did not know of from Wigan, her father's sister. Elsie was delighted to go and live with Julia, who was heavily pregnant. When she gave birth to a son not long afterwards, Elsie wept for joy, for now she had a baby 'brother' to look after – Father Christmas had made her dream come true!

I mentioned this enchanting tale on the radio one afternoon and several elderly listeners from the districts of Allerton and Calderstones said they had been told by their parents that a young lady from a well-to-do family had once lived somewhere off Yew Tree Road in Victorian times. According to folklore, she had lost her husband in tragic circumstances, and had then adopted many underprivileged and abandoned children into her home, which was said to have been a large thatched cottage.

BAFFLING BIRTH

In Liverpool, in 1920, three sisters from Parliament Street with the surname Boole, arrived the Dragon Vaults, which once stood on Brownlow Hill. At the pub, Alice, Peggy and Margaret Boole, aged twenty-two, twenty and nineteen, had come to join their father, who was enjoying a drink with his seafaring brother. It was a family affair, and many other members of the Boole family were at the pub that afternoon. There were also three young men present: William Hunter, John Lewis and James Bruce. The men soon got chatting to the lovely Boole sisters.

Not long afterwards, William Hunter started courting Alice Boole, John Lewis started courting Peggy Boole, and James Bruce, Margaret Boole. Bruce, who was of Scottish descent, stood out because his hair was a very bright shade of Titian red. All three were married on the same day that summer and the landlady of the Dragon Vaults attended the triple wedding.

By 1922, Alice Boole, who was now Alice Hunter, and Peggy Lewis, her sister, had become mothers, but their younger sister Margaret and her husband James Bruce had still not produced a child, and she yearned for a baby. In November 1922, the three husbands boarded the Cunard liner *Laconia* at the Pier Head to sail to New York, where they would hopefully find employment, and set up homes in America for their wives to join them.

The three men felt mixed emotions as they waved goodbye to their wives from the deck of the ship. Were they doing the right thing? and would they be able to build a better life for their families among the towering skyscrapers of New York? Tragically, it was one of those skyscrapers which was to claim the life of James Bruce, just one month later. Alice and Peggy heard the news first and had the task of breaking it to their little sister. With eyes brimming with tears, they knocked on her door and when they had sat her down and made her a cup of tea, they broke the news that James had been killed in a freak accident on a construction site. Margaret collapsed with the shock and when she came to, she locked herself away in her room and became a recluse, only seeing close members of her family. She would clutch at her sister's baby daughter and start to sob, rueing the fact that she would never have a child of her own.

One stormy evening, Margaret ventured out of the house on Parliament Street and wandered aimlessly up Stanhope Street. As she was passing an old Methodist chapel, a man in outdated clothes appeared out of nowhere, startling her. He gently took her hand and asked her why she was so troubled. As she listened, he led her into the chapel, where he comforted her, "Don't ever give up, a child may come." Margaret turned towards him but found herself alone. The man had seemingly evaporated into thin air, yet Margaret was suddenly transfused with an overwhelming sense of peace and optimism.

A month later, Margaret suddenly felt very poorly and a doctor was called out to examine her. He stunned both her and her sisters, when he told her that she was pregnant. She dismissed the diagnosis as nonsense, as it was thirteen months since she had slept with her late husband. Nevertheless, the doctor insisted that she was pregnant. Utterly confused, Margaret decided to get a second opinion, and the second doctor confirmed the diagnosis.

Nine months later, Margaret gave birth to a healthy baby daughter who was born with a full head of bright red hair, and her curly locks were of the same unusual shade as James

Bruce's – Titian red. News of the strange birth was vociferously contested by Bishop Chavasse of Liverpool, but Margaret's friends and family backed up her testimony, testifying that the girl had spent the last thirteen months in self-imposed isolation in her own room, in a depressed state.

To her dying day, Margaret Bruce was convinced that the man she had met on Stanhope Street had been an angel; an angel who gave her the one thing she most wanted in the world – apart from her dead husband – a child of her own.

The Strategic Reserve

I recall the night I was sleeping over at a schoolfriend's house on Smithdown Lane, in the 1970s, when I heard a dull thudding that gently shook the entire dwelling and seemed to come from the bowels of the earth. From the top of the double bunk-bed I leant over and asked what had caused the jolt. My friend seemed as startled as I was, and switched on the light, saying that his father had told him that there were tunnels running under Smithdown Lane which were haunted by a ghostly steam train and which could make the house shake. At that time, my friend was unaware of the amazing subterranean legacy of Joseph 'Mad Mole' Williamson, an eccentric from a bygone age who had riddled the sandstone bedrock of my Edge Hill neighbourhood with a system of tunnels with no obvious purpose. I had read about his labyrinth in the books of Richard Whittington Egan, and so I gradually drifted off into an uneasy sleep with imaginings of a secret city beneath the streets, populated by Victorians who had refused to die.

On the following morning, over breakfast, I mentioned

the mysterious jolt, and all conversation instantly ceased. "That'll have been that ghost train I told you about," my friend's father eventually murmured. Nothing more was said, and to this day, I do not know what rocked that house on Smithdown Lane. Surely, it could not really have been a ghostly steam train? Or could it?

Well, curiously, in recent years, the following tale came my way. Had the story originated from just one source, I would have taken it with a pinch of salt, but this account is an amalgamation of four separate people's correspondence. You may make of it what you will.

In March 1977, Tony Corbett, a scrap metal merchant, was sitting in a Sayers cafe, in Myrtle Parade, near the University campus, having a lunch break after buying a bundle of lead pipes from a local man. While scoffing his egg, beans and bacon, he thumbed through the pages of the *Daily Post* looking for the racing page. After a while he turned back a few pages to the television guide, and happened to notice the photograph of a white-haired man of about seventy-something in the corner of a page. The headline under the photo read: 'Have You Seen This Man?' The article named the man and said he had walked out of an old people's home.

Tony Corbett flipped past the page, then happened to look up and there was the old man sitting at the next table, staring at a cup of tea with a pensive look on his face. As Tony watched him, the pensioner slyly took out a small bottle of purple methylated spirits, and secretively took a sip, then stashed it away in his inside pocket. Tony approached him and pointed out his photograph in the newspaper. The old man read the article, then explained that he had decided to leave the home because he was bored stiff by the stultifying routine and lack of conversation. Mr Corbett advised him to at least telephone his relatives to put their minds at rest, but instead, he let out a string of expletives and claimed that his next of kin were hoping he would die, so they could get their hands on his money.

Corbett and the elderly man got talking, and the scrap dealer complained that he was finding it impossible to make a living and that his business was steadily folding. The old man seemed lost in thought for a while, then asked a curious question, "Do you happen own that scrap-yard by Crown Street?" Corbett nodded. The old man then confided that he knew an amazing secret about that yard which could net him a small fortune. Corbett's ears pricked up and he eagerly asked what the secret was, but the old man asked him to take him to the yard first.

Corbett had no hesitation in taking him, even though he was rather sceptical about the outcome, and when they got there, the old man scurried behind a stack of rusting car chassis and inspected a heavy iron door. It had been there for years and Corbett had assumed it provided access to the electrical transformer shed next door. The old man asked for a wire coat-hanger and Corbett eventually located one. He carefully inserted its hook into the padlock, and gently manipulated it for about a minute. Suddenly, the padlock clicked, and the old man deftly removed it – he had obviously done this before – and Corbett wondered what he had got himself into. The old man tried to pull open the door, but it wouldn't budge because the hinges were so badly rusted and he was quite frail, but Tony Corbett, being very muscular, did manage to open it. Beyond the doorway, a stone stairway led down into the darkness. The old man reached in and pressed a rubber-coated switch on the wall, and a line of bulbs behind wire-framed guards lit up the stairway. "Wait till you see this, son," he said, leading the way down the sandstone steps.

Corbett followed, wondering where they could possibly lead. After descending about five flights of steps, the two men traversed a corridor carved out of sandstone, and came upon an extraordinary sight like a deserted railway platform from long ago. Lined up on the tracks were three old steam locomotives, each in pristine condition. "Phew! Thank goodness they're still here," the old man exclaimed. He told Corbett that he had found the trains by accident about eleven years before, when he was a petty criminal, hiding stolen goods. Corbett asked who they belonged to and the old man shrugged. Perhaps the railway companies had forgotten about them and simply left them there.

Corbett knew a little about trains, and that the large locomotive in front of him belonged to the same class as the Flying Scotsman. It bore the letters LNER on its iron plating and also had a four-digit registration number on display. The second train was a turbomotive with the abbreviation LMS upon it. The two men even climbed on board the engines, which looked and felt brand new.

About forty minutes later, they climbed back up to the scrap-yard. The scrap-dealer spoke to a solicitor later that day and asked him if he could claim the trains as salvage, but he said not, as they were the property of the railways. He would have to come clean and tell the authorities. The museums would probably purchase them.

However, a strange thing happened. Government officials descended on the scene and cordoned off the scrap-yard. After interrogating Corbett at length, they said they were something to do with the Ministry of Defence, and told him to say nothing about his discovery. But the story got out anyway, and in several editions of a steam railway magazine, articles about it were printed. It transpired that the serial numbers of the secret locomotives matched those of steam trains that had not been scrapped. It was claimed that the Government had hidden away over a hundred locomotives and other transport vehicles in underground vaults and tunnels, as part of a Strategic Reserve. In the event of a serious crisis, like the aftermath of an atomic war, the coal mines would re-open, and these primitive vehicles would be brought back into operation. It was alleged that the Ministry of Defence even admitted to all this in 1979.

When a nuclear explosion occurs, a wave of intense electromagnetic energy is transmitted as a side effect, and this radiation burns out the delicate silicon chips and transistors found in modern electrical equipment, rendering hardware such as computers, radios and telephones useless. The phenomenon is known as EMP – or electromagnetic pulse effect. When the United States tested out an atomic bomb in the 1960s, it was said to have blacked out a nearby city because of EMP. A military-funded study has discovered that the only intact transport vehicles that would work after a nuclear war would be steam-driven trains, which have no delicate electrical components.

It therefore seems entirely possible that the Strategic Reserve is indeed a reality, and that the nursing home escapee had unwittingly stumbled upon one part of it.

GAS LAMP GHOUL

The following story took place in the early 1970s, at a house in the south-end of Liverpool. A man named Mike bought one of the grand old terraced houses on North Hill Street, and decided to modernise it. He began by demolishing two inside walls to create a large, spacious lounge and also had the ceiling removed and a new one put in much higher up. A huge cast iron fireplace was installed, and then, after the walls were plastered and the carpets laid, Mike's wife, Frances, thought an old authentic Victorian lamp-post in the corner would be the perfect finishing touch. Mike said it would take some trouble obtaining and fitting one, but Frances was an expert sulker, and so he put out his feelers to see if he could acquire one.

At the local pub, two brothers offered to uproot a lamp-post from Canning Street, or Rodney Street, for four hundred pounds. Mike dismissed their proposition as both ridiculous and illegal, and so decided to explore another avenue. He asked a local man, Mr Dewhurst, who had a scrap-yard in the Dingle, if he could obtain a Victorian, or Edwardian, lamp-post, and he said he could, from a friend in Warwickshire, who specialised in providing Victorian memorabilia, and who had a number of them.

Within three days, a black, cast-iron pillar, surmounted by a huge square lantern, had arrived by lorry at the house on North Hill Street. It was brought indoors and expertly installed in the lounge, and an electrician wired up a suitable soft yellow light in the housing of its lantern. Delighted with her new acquisition, Mike's wife put a ladder against the crossbar at the top of the lamp-post and climbed up to clean the four glass panes.

That night, the couple sat on their old leather sofa enjoying a glass wine and surveying their new lounge with its old lamp-post taking pride of place.

"You'd do anything for me, wouldn't you, love?" Frances said to Mike as she snuggled into his arms.

Mike was about to reply when he heard a strange, unfamiliar, musical sound.

"What was that?" asked Frances.

As they strained their ears to listen, the ornamental clock on the mantelpiece started to chime the hour of midnight. As the twelfth chime faded, they could again discern the odd jumble of tones, and both agreed that it sounded like an old-fashioned barrel-organ. It drifted into the lounge, but just as quickly diminished again. They decided, or hoped, that it had simply come from a passing car and Mike reassured her that sound travelled further at night and could play tricks on the ears.

Eventually they went to bed, and at two in the morning, their seventeen-year-old daughter, Carol, crept into the house, having just returned from a nightclub, and went straight to the fridge. She had just helped herself to a carton of milk, when she heard eerie music coming from the lounge. She spun round and was confronted by an apparition of a young man in grey old-fashioned clothes. On his head he wore a pointed white cap and his face had a ghastly purple hue. His eyes were protruding out of their sockets and his tongue was thick and black and lolled out of his mouth as if it had been wrenched out. That was disturbing enough, but what made it worse was the way his head was tilted sideways at a crazy angle – as if his neck was broken. The area around him was shrouded in shadow.

Carol threw the carton of milk at the apparition and ran

screaming out of the kitchen, through the back yard, and all the way to a friend's house. Her parents rushed from their bed upon hearing the screams and found the spilt milk all over the kitchen and the back door wide open. They ran after her and found her in a dreadful state. When she told them about the apparition, they thought she had been given LSD and had been hallucinating. They led her home and calmed her down, and she eventually went to bed at around six o'clock.

A few nights later, Frances was working late and Mike was sitting in front of the fire, doing a crossword, when he heard a fizzing sound. He looked up and saw a flickering yellow flame behind the glass panes of the lamp-post and there was the strange barrel-organ music once again, only this time he heard faint voices cheering and laughing. As he rose from his chair, the voices ended abruptly, and the jet of flame changed into an electric bulb once more.

He could not settle down again in the house on his own, so he went to pick up Frances from work. When they returned, forty minutes later, there was a police car outside the house and a gaggle of neighbours crowding round the front door. Apparently, one of them had called at the house, and peered through the blinds in the lounge, where they had seen a man hanging from the lamp-post. His body was jerking and his legs were kicking about violently. The neighbour flagged down a passing a police patrol car. The policeman also saw the hanged man, so he immediately kicked down the door, but on entering the lounge, found that the man was no longer there. The two men had both noticed the strange white pointed hat the figure wore.

Suspecting that the old lamp-post was haunted, a Catholic priest was called in to bless and exorcise the ghost, or whatever it had been, on the following afternoon.

As he carried out the ritual, an old tailor's cloth tape measure flew up from a chair and wound itself tightly around his neck, almost throttling him. Having disentangled himself, he continued his blessing and the organ music was briefly heard again. As soon as the priest had finished his work, Mike and Frances had the lamp-post removed and gave it to a scrap-dealer, who sold it to the City Council, who later used it to replace an old lamp-post on Rodney Street.

Mike and Frances spent almost four years carrying out research to establish if anyone had ever been lynched on a lamp-post in the area from where they had obtained it. They eventually discovered, through a local historian, that on 29 January 1876, a young man with learning difficulties was hanged from a lamp-post by a drunken mob down in Bedworth. During the execution, a barrel-organ had played, and hot potatoes had been sold to the bloodthirsty spectators. Mike and Frances even found an illustration of the lynching in an old edition of the *Illustrated Police News*. The hanged man wore a white pointed dunce cap, and the style of lamp-post in the drawing exactly matched the one that Mike had purchased.

TRUE COLOURS

One day I was walking along Hope Street on my way to investigate an alleged ghost sighting, when I happened to see a gang of small children happily engaged in a game of football near an alleyway on Blackburne Place. They were of different races, and it made a poignant sight, as just a few feet from where they were playing, stood the house where a racist woman once lived, many years before in the 1930s.

Grace Askworth had been brought up to believe that the colour of a person's skin determined his or her station in life. Her father had instilled the notion into her mind that white people were superior, and so by the time she reached the age of twenty-one, her prejudices were firmly set. The political situation in Britain and other parts of Europe seemed to vindicate Grace's racial views. Hitler was making his steady rise to power in Germany as he sought to 'cleanse the fatherland' of Jews, gypsies, and other ethnic minorities. Here in England, in 1932, Sir Oswald Mosley founded the British Union of Fascists, which incited violence against black and Jewish people. Members of Mosley's party wore black shirts and gave the Hitler salute.

In 1935, the women of Mosley's Fascist party went on parade in Liverpool, and Grace Askworth was one of the young people who watched the procession of women dressed in black berets, black shirts, and white calf-length skirts. Observing the parade with considerably less approval, on the other side of Blackburne Place, with a canvas bag slung across his shoulder, was Danny, a black merchant seaman of about thirty years of age. Whenever he docked in Liverpool he was given lodgings by a family in the area and had just returned from New York. In a week's time he was off on another voyage, this time to Sydney. Danny had been born in Jamaica, but at the age of six he had been brought to Liverpool by his aunt, after his parents had both died in a blazing building.

As the black-shirted women passed by, two men from the crowd who were cheering the march, spat at him. Danny had never shied away from trouble in his life and was ready to retaliate, but soon found that the rest of the mob was also against him, so, deciding that discretion was the better part of valour, he wisely backed away and made his way to the safety of his lodgings. Across the road, Grace had been inspired by the march and had decided that she would join the Fascist movement. The next day she wrote to their headquarters in London, requesting membership. Her father backed her decision wholeheartedly.

On the following day, which was a Sunday, Grace took her six-year-old niece Jemima for a walk. Jemima had long blonde flaxen hair and a perfect almost doll-like face. She had been born blind, and her world was one of scents, sounds and touch: the sensation of sunshine on her face, the faint hum of a dragonfly, the sweet aromas of the flowers in the park, things many of us never notice. On this summer afternoon, Jemima was clutching her Aunt Grace's hand as she skipped along to the corner sweetshop, when she heard the curious and comical sound of a man singing in a deep, resonant voice. She smiled and Danny, the owner of the voice, said, "I see you smiling, miss."

The girl blushed, and Grace quickly diverted her into the shop. "Come along now, Jemima. We don't talk to people like that," she said.

Danny also went in and asked for tobacco, but was sharply told to wait until the lady had been served. Grace deliberately took her time, then finally ordered a bag of boiled sweets for Jemima. Danny again politely asked for the tobacco and was begrudgingly served by the shop assistant. "Good morning," he said, as he left the shop, but received no reply.

On the pavement outside, he came upon a most distressing scene. Jemima was choking on one of the boiled sweets. She clutched her throat and was making a dreadful gagging sound as her aunt thrust her fingers into her mouth. She could not remove the sweet and Jemima sank to her knees, desperately clutching at Grace's skirts. "Somebody help!" Grace shouted. "Please, help!"

A man ran off to fetch a doctor and Danny scooped the choking girl up into his arms, as Grace protested vehemently. Jemima's body felt like a lifeless sack. Taking charge of the situation, he put his arms around the girl's waist and gently moved his fist upwards under her ribcage and squeezed. The second time he did this, the sweet was expelled from her mouth. He then gently laid the girl down and revived her by carrying out mouth to mouth resuscitation. After a few agonising minutes, in which Grace scarcely dared breathe, Jemima regained consciousness.

By the time the doctor eventually arrived, Danny was gone, and Grace realised that, in all the panic, she had forgotten to thank him. When Jemima later asked about the man who had saved her life, her grandfather told her that he had been a black man. Jemima said he was very kind and then asked innocently, "Are you a black man, Grandfather?"

Her grandfather was incensed by the question. "No! I certainly am not."

But the whole incident, and particularly Jemima's question, had made Grace Askworth see the error of her ways and how insignificant the colour of a person's skin really was. In the dark, or to a blind person, there are no different skin colours. The next day, a letter of reply came from the Fascist party and Grace immediately ripped it up and threw it on the fire. A blind girl had opened her eyes.

WHO WAS SIR PETER ROBINSON?

In the early 1860s, a dashing, yet enigmatic dandy, burst on to the high-society Liverpool scene and created a mystery that remained unsolved for generations.

One wintry evening, Sir Peter Robinson stepped out of the city's fog-bound streets like some spectre without a past and entered, uninvited, into a soirée, where he captivated the guests and set many female pulses racing with his youthful good looks and athletic physique. He introduced himself as Lord Loxley, and not a single person bothered to consult the pages of *Burke's Peerage* to check whether Sir Peter was indeed one of noble descent.

Within seven calendar months, Lord Loxley had disappeared as mysteriously as he had come. The fascination which the vanished nobleman left in his wake was as intense as the intrigue which surrounded the disappearance of Lord Lucan a hundred years later. For many years, people in the upper echelons of Liverpudlian society debated what had become of him. Theories abounded. Was he a phantom? perhaps the Devil in a top hat and coat tails? For even when he was regularly seen in the city, no one had ever discovered exactly where Sir Peter lived, or from whence he came. Was he a foreign spy? the illegitimate offspring of a royal? a polished charlatan? What follows is the truthful answer, which was divulged to me by a descendant of the 'Lord'.

In January 1862, Charlotte 'Lottie' Watkins, who was just sixteen, noticed a small card in the parlour window of a house on Duke Street which read: 'Parlourmaid wanted – thoroughly able to clean silver plate, wait well, and have an ability for plain needlework. Good personal character and references essential. Apply within.'

Lottie obtained references from a previous employer and returned to the house in her Sunday best. She was admitted by Mr Chivers, a very old and decrepit servant, and ushered into the drawing room, where a very frail and sick-looking woman, Mrs Ransom, interviewed her. The interview was successful and Lottie was subsequently hired.

Not long afterwards, a vacancy arose for a servant to replace Chivers, who was about to retire, so Lottie suggested her elder brother, George Watkins, who held a boring and poorly paid job in a tobacconist's on Richmond Row. To Lottie's delight, George was hired. George and Lottie took over the care of Mrs Ransom, whose health quickly deteriorated to such an extent that she ended up confined to bed. A doctor visited and told the servants that, since her husband's death six months previously, Mrs Ransom had gone into a decline and he advised complete bed rest. This gave George and Lottie the run of the house, since doddery Mr Chivers now rarely ventured up the long flights of stairs to visit his mistress, his health being almost as bad as hers.

One evening, George Watkins went missing, and Lottie eventually found him in an elegant, second-floor room which the late Mr Ransom had used as his dressing-room. He was posing before a full-length mirror, dressed in a silken top hat, Inverness cape and long chequered coat. In his left hand he twirled a walking stick with an ornate silver handle and Lottie also noticed an impressive ring, set with a large scarlet bloodstone. With a flourish, the cheeky teenager then applied a monacle to his left eye as a finishing touch. Georgie looked quite the dandy as he studied his reflection from every angle in the enormous mahogany mirror, and complimented his reflection in a mock high-class accent.

Lottie was totally shocked: "Take those clothes off at once, George. Just who do you think you are?"

"Why, I am Sir Peter Robinson, Lord Loxley, my dear!" Georgie replied, in a passably well-spoken voice. He possessed an amazing talent for imitation, and had 'stolen' the voice from a well-to-do customer who had frequented the Everton tobacconist's. Lottie couldn't suppress a giggle as he paraded about the room having imaginary conversations with members of the gentry and even the Queen herself! That should have been the end of the joke, but that night, the top-hatted Georgie Watkins departed the Duke Street house and strolled through the foggy night in his borrowed finery. Policemen saluted him, and even the ladies of the night on Paradise Street propositioned him with the utmost deference. After some time walking about in this way, Georgie was returning to Duke Street, when an old vagrant approached him and asked if he could spare a few farthings. "I cannot, sir," Georgie said, because he carried no money.

The tramp smiled knowingly, "Someone high-falutin' like you with no money? Strikes me as a bit odd, sir, but I'll bid you goodnight."

Taking care that he was not being observed, Georgie rushed round to the tradesman's entrance and sidled into the Duke Street house, where he changed his clothes in the dressing room. It had been such a thrill to impersonate one of the elite, and he lay in bed that night going over the night's events in his mind and planning his next exploit.

Days later, a letter from the Lord Mayor inviting Mrs Ransom and a friend to a ball at the town hall, arrived at the house. She was far too ill to contemplate such an outing, so Georgie decided that Sir Peter Robinson should go instead. He inspected the card which had accompanied the letter, and saw that it didn't name a particular person, so he went along brimming with self confidence. Sir Peter Robinson was cordially received by the Lord Mayor, and every woman, young and old, was fascinated by the mysterious young man. He was an exceptionally good dancer and everyone watched with admiration as he energetically danced the polka and waltzed elegantly about the hall.

Champagne flowed, and 'Sir Peter's' behaviour became increasingly outrageous. He brazenly carried a merchant's wife out on to a balcony and kissed her passionately in front of her husband. The infuriated fellow protested vehemently, upon which Sir Peter challenged him to a duel, but the merchant backed off, grumbling that the nobility thought they were above the law.

That night, inside the string of carriages leaving the town hall, all the revellers were talking about the dashing, yet impudent newcomer. Men, whilst publicly protesting about his shocking behaviour, secretly wished they could be as audacious as him, and many women secretly desired him as a lover. A special carriage was laid on for Sir Peter to carry him to his Duke Street residence, where he arrived so full of champagne he could barely stand, and once the carriage had trundled off, he staggered stealthily to the tradesman's entrance in the alleyway. Once more, he came upon the old tramp lurking in the alley. Feeling generous because of the drink, he brought him into the kitchen and they sat down and ate supper together. The tramp openly questioned George's ancestry, saying that he knew he was nothing more than a servant, but seemed to see the funny side of the deception. He assured him that his secret was safe and after supper, he left, full of gratitude. He was invited into the kitchen on several more occasions and became a friend of both George and Lottie Watkins.

By July, Sir Peter Robinson was the talk of the town, and people vied with each other to have him their guest. On one occasion he was invited to a lavish ball at the Adelphi Hotel, where he met Mohammed Said, the Viceroy of Egypt, and the Lord Mayor, who was now on first name terms with 'Sir Peter'. Also attending the ball was a small round portly man with a large moustache, which merged with his fashionable long side whiskers, or 'Piccadilly Weepers' as they were called. This man, who looked tantalisingly familiar to Georgie, was introduced to him as Mr Arthur Vincent, a retired judge and colonel, who had been wounded at the Battle of Balaclava in the Crimean War. Georgie listened as Mr Vincent talked about his blood-curdling exploits in the Crimea to a circle of fascinated men and women.

Later on, Mr Vincent confronted George in a secluded corner and in a hushed tone said, "You, sir, are a fake!" George bravely kept up the pretence, despite a sickening churning in his stomach, and threatened to sue Mr Vincent for slander. The fat old raconteur was having none of it. "You are no more a lord than the man in the moon! You work in a tobacconist's shop on Richmond Row," he growled.

Georgie's heart skipped a beat. Now he knew why Mr Vincent had looked so familiar – he regularly used to serve him tobacco. In whispers, Mr Vincent interrogated the young impostor, and that night, after the party, he travelled to the Ransom household with George to make the necessary arrangements for blackmail. The stipulation was that Georgie would pay out several guineas each week to Mr Vincent, or the police would be informed of the grave offence of impersonating a lord. Arthur Vincent was sitting in the kitchen, smugly sipping a large brandy, when in walked Lottie with the old tramp. When Mr Vincent saw the tramp his jaw dropped. After a long silence, the tramp said, "Well, well! Look who it is! Mr Percy Lilly, or lily-livered Lilly as we used to call him."

Mr Vincent shot to his feet and stumbled backwards in shock, knocking over a chair. "How dare you, you impertinent fellow! What are you doing in a house such as this? Get out this minute, or I will call the constabulary."

"You're mistaken; his name isn't Lilly, it's Vincent," said George. "He's a retired judge."

"Yes, and I'm the Prince of Wales," said the tramp. "He's no retired judge, he's a deserter!"

A pallid Mr Vincent quickly quit the kitchen without a word. Maybe it was the shock he had suffered that night, or just natural causes, but days afterwards, he collapsed and later died at the Royal Infirmary, where his true identity was soon established. The doctors found a blue letter 'D' tattooed on his arm, the mark of a deserter, inscribed there by an army doctor. His name had indeed been Percy Lilly.

Georgie's recent fun and games lost their appeal after this narrow escape, so he carefully replaced all of the late Mr Ransom's finery and never dressed up as a lord again. But for years afterwards, at upper class parties and gatherings, guests would speculate as to what had become of that dashing young bachelor, Sir Peter Robinson.

THE BOOK OF PROVERBS

In December 2000, John Reece, a fifty-five-year-old Aigburth businessman, was casually perusing through various old-fashioned tomes in an antiquarian bookshop, when he happened to come upon a beautiful wine-coloured, leather-bound Victorian diary for the year 1889. There were no entries or notes written in the diary; it had never been used. On some of the dates, the diary gave information about sunrise, sunset, the phases of the moon, bank holidays, saints' feast days, Ash Wednesday and so forth. Also, on certain dates, there were proverbs and sayings printed in italics; a sort of 'thought for the day'. Mr Reece bought the diary for three pounds and took it home.

On New Year's Day 2002, he realised that the diary of 1889 corresponded exactly with the days and dates of the year 2002, so he decided to use it for the year ahead. He jotted down the days when he would be off work in January, and as he turned to the page for the 17th and 18th of that month, he noticed that there were a couple of proverbs corresponding to them. The first was morbid: 'Death surprises us in the midst of our hopes.' The second read: 'The course of true love never did run smooth.' On the first of those two dates, Harry, a close friend of Reece's, dropped dead in the parlour of his local pub. Ironically, Harry had just been telling John Reece that he had been to the doctor, and that his usually high blood pressure was now back to normal, and he had also been carefully watching his diet. Just a few seconds later, he collapsed from heart failure and landed at his friend's feet. John Reece later thought about that day's proverb and shuddered. Must have been a coincidence, he thought, despite a feeling of slight unease.

On the following day, he bumped into an old flame of his called Barbara, and persuaded her to go to a wine bar on Lark Lane with him, where they ended up reminiscing about old times. Several glasses of wine later, John and Barbara were holding hands and thoroughly enjoying each other's company. Barbara went home with him, but that night, John said something to upset her. He made a flippant remark and Barbara slapped his face and left. He later looked at the old diary for that date, and re-read the quotation: 'The course of true love never did run smooth'. That had to be a coincidence as well – surely?

With thoughts of trying to win back Barbara weighing heavily on his mind, Reece flipped through the pages of the diary and they fell open at Thursday, 14 February, St Valentine's Day. The proverb for the only date in the calendar associated with love, was appropriately printed in red and declared: 'Opportunity seldom knocks twice'. This set John wondering. Should he grasp the moment and ask Barbara to be his wife? He decided that it may well have some significance and resolved to propose to her on that date, rather than perhaps miss the opportunity forever.

On Valentine's Day then, Reece made arrangements to take Barbara to a top class restaurant. He meticulously prepared for the evening, spending ages in the bathroom, dressing in his most expensive suit and finally splashing on a generous dose of aftershave. He looked anxiously again at the engagement ring he had bought – a blue sapphire set in platinum, which had cost him two thousand pounds. As he was preparing to leave for Barbara's home, his telephone started to ring, but, not wanting to be late, he quickly switched on his answering machine and from it, he heard the voice of his friend Mike, who lived down in Wrexham. A hackney cab sounded its horn outside. "Sorry, Mike," he said to himself, as he anxiously glanced at his watch. He left the house in a hurry, purposely turning off his mobile as he entered the taxi. Nothing was going to interrupt his plans, which he hoped would mark the end of his bachelorhood.

At the restaurant, Barbara was acting strangely. She appeared distant, as if something was weighing heavily on her mind. Towards the end of the meal, which John thought had gone very well, he plucked up courage and said, "Barbara, I want to ask you a very important question, and I think you know what the question is going to be." He took the small velvet box from his pocket and placed it on the table in front of her. She said nothing and her eyes closed for a while. When they opened, they were glassy with tears. John thought she was crying because she was so overcome by the impending proposal. However, when she did start to speak, Barbara said she had only come on the date to tell him something important. She had met a man several months ago, and intended to marry him. She would have been spending Valentine's Day with him, but he was working down in London. She had thought it would be fitting to use the date to let John know that he was still a friend, and a very good one at that, but she felt no love for him anymore. If she had known he had intended to propose, she would never have come.

John was devastated, and in a choked voice, said, "You decided to tell me on this day of all days? I'll never understand the mind of a woman."

Barbara was upset and embarrassed and quickly left, saying she was sorry.

When John Reece got home he listened to the messages

on his answering machine. His Wrexham friend said he urgently needed twenty thousand pounds to put into a business opportunity that had arisen unexpectedly. A bistro with amazing prospects had come on the market, and Mike needed twenty thousand pounds to seal a business arrangement which would make him the owner of the bistro, which was located in a popular area of Dublin. Mike called back four times that evening, and on the fourth call he told John that the money had now been put up by another friend. That bistro is now flourishing and Mike is set to open up another in Ireland. John Reece quickly realised that, once again, the old diary had seemingly forewarned him about his lost chance with the proverb, 'Opportunity seldom knocks twice'.

From that time onwards, John Reece became obsessed with the diary and its proverbs. He flipped through the pages, reading each of them and one in particular, for July, made his blood run cold. Its stark message read, 'The best go first'. What could this possibly mean? Would he lose someone close to him on that date? Sure enough, when the date arrived, John Reece heard that his best friend, who had emigrated to Australia many years before, had been knocked down and killed near his home in Sydney.

It could all be dark coincidence, or perhaps that diary of long ago really did have the power to foretell the future.

LIFE STORY

I first heard this unusual tale many years ago, and several people who personally knew the man who is the subject of the story have backed it up with their own accounts.

Around 1958, forty-five-year-old Tommy MacIntyre went to visit his seven-year-old daughter Susan in the Children's Hospital in Myrtle Street, where she was due to have her adenoids removed. Tommy was separated from his wife. He was a drunkard and a bully, who had left her black and blue on more than one occasion, so she had finally left him and taken their daughter with her to a house in Devonshire Road, in Toxteth. Tommy told his little girl she would be fine, and hugged and kissed her, then left the hospital and walked straight into the Mulberry Bush. There he downed three pints, then went on to the Red House on the corner of Crown Street, where he knocked back several shots of rum in quick succession. As usual, he quickly became bellicose, and after threatening a fellow drinker, was ejected him from the premises.

Tommy McIntyre then turned up at the Bear's Paw, in Paddington, where he was involved in yet another altercation. From there he staggered to the Weighing Machine, on Wavertree Road, where he threatened to throw a bar stool through the jukebox, because the music was not to his liking. Once again he was thrown out of the pub. Within half an hour, McIntyre was causing a disturbance at the Leigh Arms, but even after two men roughly escorted him outside and threw him on to the pavement, he was still hungry for trouble.

Minutes later, on the Wavertree High Street, McIntyre made the mistake of calling two well-built Teddy Boys "big girls' blouses", because of their outlandish attire. They gave him a pasting and left him bleeding and bruised on Pye Street. With a bloodied nose, a black eye and a ripped jacket, Tommy crawled down an alleyway which came out on Prince Alfred Road and took refuge in what looked like a music hall. There was no one in the small foyer, so he walked into the dark auditorium unchallenged, and flopped down on a comfortable seat, nursing his bruised limbs. Not another soul was about. The lights suddenly dimmed, and a projector whirred behind him. A powerful beam of light cut through the air and a film was projected on to the screen.

Even in his drunken, battered state, Tommy realised that he must have wandered into a cinema, albeit a very strange one. A silent film with no titles or credits commenced. The first scene showed a vaguely familiar building, which Tommy soon realised was the infants' school he had attended long ago. Then his heart jumped as crowds of children poured into the street and filed through the arched entrance to the school with their mothers.

One boy and his mother remained at the entrance and the film showed a close-up of them. The boy was crying and his mother was wiping his tears away and smiling. He didn't want to go to school. That boy was Tommy MacIntyre! Tommy's addled brain sluggishly tried to fathom it out. If it was a dream, Tommy, filled with nostalgia, hoped he would not wake up for a while. Tears blurred his vision as he watched his loving mother trying to get him to let go of her hand on his first day at school.

Breathtaking scenes of forgotten memories, long-dead friends and long-demolished places were screened in vivid monochrome. There was his loyal old mongrel dog Blacky that he had thought would live forever, running alongside him. As a young Tommy Mac turned the dog's ears inside out, the Tommy of 1958 wiped away his tears and laughed as Blacky violently shook his head.

Then came another scene that had long been lost to memory – a scene which broke his heart – the moment when he found his grandmother lying dead in her armchair. He watched the nine-year-old Tommy shaking her, trying to wake her up. Suddenly, the hurt in Tommy's heart made the aches and pains from the beating seem insignificant. The young Tommy lay across his beloved gran, sobbing silently as Blacky tilted his head – his brown eyes puzzled and sorrowful.

The next scene was equally painful – his first love, at the tender age of thirteen. Kate had drifted into his life in the summer of 1926. They had planned to run away together but she ended up falling for another boy. Tommy felt the sadness welling up in his chest as he watched the pretty girl on the screen. All of the key moments, all of the golden memories of his life were shown, nothing was spared: the scenes where he saw his wife's face for the first time and the close-ups of his daughter's birth. His emotions were in turmoil and he howled out, "Stop it! Stop it! I don't want to see any more, I can't stand it!" But the invisible projectionist paid no heed to his cries. Graphic scenes of him beating his wife in a drunken rage; three-year-old Susan running into her bedroom and hiding under the blankets; close-ups of the blood on his wife's face, her tears ... not to mention all the friends whom Tommy had driven away through constant drunken arguments and fights.

Then came the terrifying scene depicting the end result of all the drinking – a funeral – his funeral. He saw the wake, with his own bloodless corpse wrapped in a white shroud and his little girl, dressed in black, crying.

At this point, the film ended as mysteriously as it had begun. The whirring of the projector died away and a deathly hush fell on the empty auditorium. Tommy rushed outside and made his way to his brother's house in a highly emotional state. He babbled out a fragmented account of the eerie film of his own life – and death. His brother Alfie tried to calm him down and after listening to his incredible story, reassured him that the 'film' was probably a product of the DTs, and anyway, there was no cinema on that road. Tommy was not to be shaken from his belief that he definitely had been in a cinema, DTs or no DTs.

Realising that things had reached crisis point, Alfie knew that he would have to help his brother, or he was doomed. With his support, Tommy became a changed man. It didn't happen overnight, of course, and it certainly wasn't easy, but he did improve himself sufficiently to renew his wedding vows about a year later and turn himself into a decent husband and father.

Minutes after I broadcast an account of this story on the radio, several older listeners rang in to say that there had indeed been a cinema on Prince Alfred Road in the days of black and white films, but it had been demolished around 1950. It was called The Magnet, and it stood next to the Prince Alfred pub. The cinema had therefore once stood on the exact spot where Tommy McIntyre, a violent drunkard, facing oblivion, was shown the story of his life and given a stark warning of what lay ahead, unless he rid himself of his ruinous addiction.

A Bridge Too Far

On the Friday night of 20 September 2001, forty-nine-year-old Tony left his home in Speke and drove in his transit van to his mother's house in the Windmill Hill area of Runcorn, where he was to spend the weekend decorating. On Sunday, at around seven in the evening, he drove up to Halton Road to his cousin's, to borrow a ladder to complete the work. He loaded up the ladder, plus a few pots of exterior paint, then set off to his mother's at about 8.15pm.

Fifteen minutes into the journey, Tony received a frantic call on his mobile from his thirteen-year-old daughter Christina. Her mum was being violently sick and was doubled up with stomach pains. She had already called for an ambulance. He called his mother and told her what had happened and returned home immediately. At this point, Tony was somewhere near Boston Avenue, and it was here that events took a very strange turn.

In extreme situations, many of us do stupid things. We push at doors that say 'pull' and can even forget our own names, addresses and telephone numbers. In Tony's case, it was dark and he was never too familiar with the Runcorn area at the best of times. So it was no surprise that he lost his bearings after getting caught up in slow moving traffic and made the mistake which many motorists make – he decided to take a short cut, and ended up going in the opposite direction. Getting more and more desperate, he swore at the confusing road signs and decided to try another route; a decision that brought him face-to-face with something that will baffle him for years to come.

He came upon a modern, enormously long, unfamiliar bridge, which seemed to be located about half a mile east of

Runcorn Bridge and, anyway, didn't have the distinctive arched hump for a start. It was straight and very long, probably about one and a half miles in total. The strangest thing of all was that there was not a single vehicle on this new bridge, which consisted of two dual carriageways going in opposite directions. Tony cagily drove on to the bridge, hoping that it wasn't still under construction, but by this time he was so beside himself that he didn't think about that too much. At one point he looked down and saw a canal of some sort – perhaps the Manchester Ship Canal.

When he left the bridge, he found himself on a stretch of motorway that eventually led him on to another road network. At this point, he stopped to ask a motorist for directions, and when he told the driver he had taken the wrong bridge, he received a blank stare. There was only one bridge across the Mersey, the motorist told him. Eventually, Tony reached Speke, where he stopped to call Christina. She didn't answer but a neighbour did, and told him that she and her mother were in the hospital, where his wife was being operated on for acute appendicitis.

His wife later made a full recovery, at which point a very relieved Tony began thinking again about the night she was admitted to hospital, and particularly about the mysterious bridge. He soon returned to the area to try and satisfy himself that, despite all evidence to contrary, such a bridge actually existed. Of course, there was no such bridge.

Completely bewildered by the experience, he contacted me and I told him that in the year 2000, I had received a call from a Halton woman who had also seen a ghostly bridge spanning the Mersey at that point, which she estimated to be about a mile east of the original Runcorn Bridge. Perhaps the spectral bridge is a glimpse of a future bridge that is often talked about, but which has yet to be built.

In December 2000, the *Daily Post* reported that Halton Borough Council had appointed Chester-based engineering consultants, Gifford, to carry out feasibility studies for a new bridge across the River Mersey to ease congestion. An artist's impression of the new one hundred and fifty million pound bridge in the newspaper, pictured the crossing about half a mile east of the current bridge. The bridge was straight and flat, without the distinctive hump of the present day bridge.

BLACK MARY

Around 1989, in a window in a Bold Street shop that sold fine art, I once saw a beautiful oil painting by an obscure Lancashire artist from the Victorian period, William Osbert. Set in what was said to be Sefton Park, the subject of the painting was a palm reader who looked like the archetypal female gypsy of popular imagination, complete with colourful headscarf and large gold loop earrings. Her face was dark, her green eyes large and mysterious, and surrounding the Romany mystic was a circle of well-to-do bonneted ladies carrying parasols. One of these ladies was having her palm read. The title of the work was 'Palm-reading Sunday'. It was dated 1873, the year after the park had been officially opened by Prince Arthur. I inquired about the background to the painting, but the man in the art shop could tell me nothing beyond the fact that the work had been discovered several years previously at the house of a reclusive old woman on Charles Berrington Road in Wavertree.

One day I was gazing at the painting once again in the window, when an old man stopped beside me and peered at the same work. He complained that the sun would fade the painting and that it ought to be placed in the shop's shady interior. I agreed, and the man started to reel off some amazing tales about the scene depicted in the painting. He told me that the palmist was a Hungarian named Mary Strang, who had been paid a guinea by William Osbert to pose for the portrait.

Mary Strang's predictions were so accurate and uncanny, that the Church and the authorities soon banned her from reading fortunes in Sefton Park, where, in the summer, she was accustomed to reading the delicate palms of ladies out on their Sunday strolls. She was very swarthy, with long black hair and knowing green eyes and had the reputation of being able to see into people's minds and many avoided her because she could read their darkest desires and innermost secrets.

In the early 1890s, Mary upset a certain affluent Liverpool family by claiming that they were all cursed and would die terrible deaths because their ancestors had driven the poor people of Ireland out of their homes to die of starvation. Strangely enough, within a very short time, each member of that family started to die, one by one. The youngest died from scarlet fever, soon followed by his mother after a riding accident. The deaths continued until only the daughter was left and she was placed in the care of relatives.

Black Mary, as Mary Strang was known, went on to make a very controversial accusation which ruffled the feathers of high class society. It took place on St George's Plateau, in Lime Street, where Mary was selling artificial flowers and noticed a well dressed gentleman approaching the entrance to St George's Hall. When she offered him an imitation carnation, the man allegedly struck out with his walking cane, rapping her hand quite sharply. She yelled out in pain, then, closing her eyes and concentrating very hard, accused him of committing several serious and sexual offences. The man, who happened to be Sir Leslie Stephen (brother of the celebrated Judge Stephen, who had sentenced Florence Maybrick to death at St George's Hall) turned purple with rage. He immediately fetched a policeman and had Mary thrown into the cells under St George's Hall, without a hearing, or official arrest.

There may have been some truth in Mary Strang's accusations, because Sir Leslie Stephen should have reported the woman for defamation of character and slander, but he decided instead to use his connections at St George's Hall, and had her put in one of the dingiest cells in the bowels of the hall. He probably only intended to confine her for a few days, but she became seriously ill, and died soon afterwards, but not before she uttered a chilling curse.

Judge Stephen and his younger brother heard through the grapevine that the gypsy had put a curse of death upon Sir Leslie, claiming that he would be plagued by illness until his death. Shortly afterwards, and for the rest of his life, he suffered dizzy spells, which left him nauseous and even the most eminent Harley Street doctors could find no cause for his perplexing symptoms. He died a slow agonising death, and his body had a look of absolute terror on its face. For hours on his deathbed he had rambled on about the accursed Mary Strang, so many believed that her deadly curse had truly come to pass.

Days after Black Mary's death, her ghost was seen roaming the cells of St George's Hall, and she even put in an appearance in the law courts. Many people who have worked at St George's Hall assure me that Mary's shade continues to haunt the place from time to time.

THE RETURN OF WALTER SLIM

A former student of the University of Liverpool once rang me to relate a story I had heard something of before. I often hear several versions of an alleged supernatural event, and more often than not, I have to try and iron out a number of inconsistencies. The following story, however, was related to me over a period of almost three years, from no fewer than seven people, and all of their recollections concurred entirely. The last piece of the jigsaw, which made the story complete, was the discovery of a name in a Liverpool cemetery which I happened to stumble upon. Without further ado, here is the eerie tale of Walter Slim.

On the evening of Friday 13 August 1971, at around nine o'clock, five male students left their lodgings on Liverpool's Upper Stanhope Street and headed for the Philharmonic pub on Hope Street. This was the so-called 'glam rock' era, with bands like T Rex appearing in the pop charts, and it was not unusual for the youth of the day, especially students, to dress outlandishly. Two of the five students wore battered old top hats and Army trench-coats, and one wore a deerstalker with a scarlet carnation. They agreed to take a short cut through St James's cemetery next to the Anglican Cathedral, a creepy place even in broad daylight, but this was nine o'clock at night, and twilight had heightened the feeling of menace in the vast graveyard. They were glad when they had emerged unscathed on the far side of the cemetery, and hurried past the Liverpool Institute (which is now the Fame School, LIPA).

One of the students, Douggie, noticed someone walking

alongside them, wearing a top hat, a long black opera cloak, a white starched collar and a large bow tie. He was about six feet tall and aged about thirty. His face was extremely anaemic-looking and Douggie nudged one of his friends, and grimaced, "Who's he?" His friend sneaked a look at the stranger and shrugged.

The students crossed Hardman Street but the stranger stood rooted to the kerb, gazing in apparent fascination at the cars waiting at the traffic lights. Douggie and his friends entered the spacious lounge of the Philharmonic, which was packed on this Friday night. As Douggie was ordering a drink, the top-hatted man dashed into the pub, threw back his cloak and screeched with laughter. He looked demented, or possibly high on drugs. The barman looked him up and down and asked him what he wanted to drink, and in a weird voice he replied, "In the name of human charity, I'll have your gin, sir!" The barman asked how he wanted the gin, and the man impatiently waved his hand and shouted, "Gin, sir! Nothing else!" and slapped the counter three times with the palm of his hand.

Everyone backed off, because there was something extremely threatening about the man. A lot of people later recalled how he had given off an awful body odour, mingled with a sickly sweet scent, reminiscent of violets. The glass of gin was duly poured and placed before him, and the barman held out his hand, expecting to be paid, but the stranger ignored him, swigging down the neat, undiluted gin and banging the glass down on the counter.

He then turned around and walked to a corner where a black girl was standing on her own. She was exceptionally beautiful and wore her hair in the popular 'Afro' style. She backed up against the wall as the malodorous individual approached. He grabbed her hand, kissed her knuckle and tilted his hat. "My name is Walter Slim," he said, and his dark eyes seemed to smile, though his lips did not move. He asked the girl her name.

"Sarah," she said, self-consciously.

"What a delightful name!" Walter chimed, and began to ramble on about how his father had supported the campaign to end the despicable institution of slavery. He then lapsed into sentimentality, and in a choked-up voice, said, "Many, many years ago, I loved a girl named Sarah. The beautiful Miss Sarah Beaton." He then produced an exquisite silver locket and opened it to show Sarah the oval portrait of a young golden-haired lady. He became melancholy as he described how she had died from a fever, just days before he was due to marry her. She had been just seventeen. The twentieth century Sarah felt great sympathy for the smelly stranger and subconsciously knew he must be some sort of flesh and blood ghost. Strangely, she was no longer afraid.

"I feel quite ill," Walter announced suddenly.

At this point, the barman who had been diddled out of his payment told him to get out, adding that he was permanently barred. Walter stumbled out of the pub into the night, with Sarah following him. Her friends begged her not to go after him, because he was obviously mad, but she ignored them. She followed him to the cemetery nestling in the shadow of the Gothic splendour of the massive Anglican Cathedral, and immediately noticed how he seemed terrified of the traffic plying its way along Rodney Street. She squinted into the darkness and watched him stagger off until he could no longer be seen. She was afraid of the dark and wisely decided against going into the cemetery alone.

Well, that should have been that. The incident went

down in Liverpool folklore; the far-fetched tale of Walter Slim, the Victorian ghost who called in for a gin at the Philharmonic pub, had even reached my young ears when I was a child living off nearby Myrtle Street. Some thought the visitation was a hoax, staged by some madcap student with a dark sense of humour on that Friday the thirteenth.

Then, one evening in July 2002, I was in the Everyman Bistro when I happened to meet a man named Ken, who had once been a photographer for the *Liverpool Echo* many years before. We chatted on the subject of the paranormal, and Ken mentioned that he had once been called out to take a photograph of a huge, eight-pointed, occult symbol, which black magicians had drawn in the cellar of the derelict John Bagot Hospital in the north of the city. The dabblers in the Black Arts had drawn up the symbol in the old hospital, because so many people had died there over the years, and they probably wanted to try and channel the energy that had been released at that location to open up a portal to demonic entities.

Ken later produced the actual photograph. I had seen the strange symbols somewhere before. I checked them against a photograph I had in my possession of an identical eight-pointed star scrawled in the desecrated tomb of a Victorian gentleman in the Cathedral cemetery off Hope Street, in 1971. I checked the name on this tomb, it read: 'Walter Slim, 1861-1888'. He had died at the tender age of twenty-seven. I then remembered the old tale about the ghost walking into the Philharmonic. The other name he mentioned. I located Sarah's grave in the same cemetery. She had died in 1885, aged seventeen.

The occultists who had broken into Walter Slim's tomb had carried out one of the most controversial and terrifying rituals in black magic, the 'Octagenesis of Resurrection', which is purported to be a way of raising the dead. However, the revived corpse usually disintegrates after an hour or so. Only perfectly preserved corpses, taken from a lead-lined coffin, are used in the ritual. Walter Slim had been laid to rest in just such a lead coffin ...

HAVE WE MET SOMEWHERE BEFORE?

In October 1995, Janet, a twenty-five-year-old St Helen's woman, broke up with her boyfriend after she discovered he had been having an affair. The break-up left her feeling very low and so her friends decided to do something to get her back to her normal chirpy self. Late one evening, Janet and her two friends were listening to a lonely hearts radio programme entitled *Evening Encounter*, which involved listeners writing in to presenter Pete Price with their personal details and the type of man or woman they were looking for etc. The listeners who liked the sound of what they heard would write in and a meeting would be arranged with an eye to romance.

On this particular night, the presenter read out a touching letter from a girl called Janet, who was twenty-five, and lived in the St Helen's area. Having just broken up with her boyfriend, she wanted to meet a considerate and loving man in the Merseyside area who would take her out, and also spend cosy nights in with her. Janet's heart skipped a beat when she heard all this, because she realised it was referring to herself, and that it had been written by her two giggling friends whose voices she immediately recognised, and who had obviously decided to play Cupid.

The response to the letter was good. About five days later, twenty-two letters arrived at the radio station, and were passed on to Janet. In a fit of giggles, she and her friends read through them, and they all agreed that the most promising one was from thirty-two-year-old Murray, from Knowsley. He had enclosed a passport-type photograph and seemed quite handsome ... and strangely familiar. She telephoned Murray and they spent ages talking before arranging to meet in person at a pub in St Helens. Janet felt very peculiar when they met, convinced she had met him somewhere before, and the strange thing was that Murray later said he had felt the same, but couldn't say where.

The couple walked across the lounge bar and Murray pointed to two vacant chairs at a table near a blazing log fire, but, with considerable embarrassment, Janet told him she could not sit there, as she had suffered from a fear of fire all her life. He was very understanding and sat in the corner and told her that he had a psychological hang-up over fire as well, only it was not a phobia – it was a mania. When he was a child, he had developed pyromania – a fixation with burning things. A lot of boys have this fixation at that age, but Murray was sent to a child psychiatrist because, at the age of seven, he had gathered together all his sister's dolls and then burned them in a heap in the back yard. Even more alarmingly, he had also set fire to a girl's hair at school. He laughed off these incidents, but all the talk of fire made Janet shudder.

Despite sharing this hang-up, they continued to see one another, and a few days later, went to a Halloween party. Janet dressed as a witch, complete with pointed hat and a long black Gothic dress. On seeing her outfit, Murray flipped and his usually sociable personality underwent a drastic change. "You shouldn't have dressed like that," he said ominously. "What did you think you were doing?"

"Why, what's the matter with it?" Janet asked,

crestfallen. "It's only a bit of fun."

"I can't stand witches, that's all. They make my stomach churn. They're evil. They should stop all this Halloween nonsense, it goes against God."

"For goodness sake, Murray, lighten up. It's a fancy dress party," said Janet. "I thought my outfit was spot on," and she leaned over to kiss him, but he seemed cold and distant all of a sudden.

Days later, Murray was driving Janet to a bonfire night party, and as the car passed a field where a bonfire was blazing, Janet covered her face with her hands, because she was terrified of the way the crackling flames flickered across the children's faces, as they jeered at the smouldering Guy. Murray, meanwhile, slowed down the car and wound down the window to get a better view of the impressive bonfire. He revelled, wide eyed, at the odours of charred wood, and marvelled at how clean the flames seemed, how they seemed to sterilise, then devour, whatever they touched. Janet yelled for him to drive on and eventually he did so.

At the party, Janet and Murray were introduced to a man who was training to be a hypnotherapist. He claimed that he could remove any phobia through hypnotic regression. He would put a person in a trance using hypnosis, then dredge through their subconscious to find the root cause of the phobia. He hypnotised Janet, and asked her why she hated fire so much. Under hypnosis she vividly remembered being an old woman who was burned to death! She remembered her head being shaved, and a man pouring something flammable on to her scalp and back and then setting it alight. He put her in a large barrel and the brushwood around the barrel was also lit with a torch. She was a witch named Janet, being burnt alive. All about her, she could see the laughing, jeering faces, distorted by the flames and intense, shimmering heat. One of those faces was all too familiar – it was Murray! It was he that held the flaming torch. At that point, Janet passed out from the agony of the searing flames and found herself in total darkness and absolute silence.

The startled hypnotherapist quickly lifted the trance and Janet was carried to a sofa, where she gradually recovered from the difficult, but illuminating, ordeal. The hypnotherapist later suggested hypnotising Murray, to see if he had actually been some sort of witchfinder in a previous life, but he sternly declined, saying hypnotism was the work of the Devil.

About a year later, Murray and Janet were touring in Scotland on holiday, when they passed through a place called Dornoch. They both found that they somehow knew every inch of the area, even though neither had never been there before. Janet experienced an over-powering sensation that this was the place where she had been burnt at the stake in a previous life. They decided to explore the place and Murray came upon an unusual stone inscribed with the date 1727. A tourist was taking photographs of the stone and Janet asked him what event the boulder marked. The tourist turned out to be very well informed and told them that a witch called Janet Horne had been burnt to death in a barrel of oil on that spot in 1727 – the last witch to be burned in Scotland. The account so closely matched Janet's experience under hypnosis, that she immediately felt faint, especially when she heard the name Janet Horne.

She later researched the witch-burning incident and discovered that Janet Horne had had her head shaved and then been doused with brandy. The flames would cleanse her soul before death, the witchfinders had announced.

Murray later confessed that he had suffered vivid nightmares of flames burning Janet, but in the dreams, she had been much older.

Not surprisingly, the couple later split up, believing that in a previous existence, they had been murderer and victim.

JIGSAW JINX

What follows was related to me by a Mrs Bryant and has been known in her family for generations. It concerns Mrs Bryant's grandfather, George Ratcliffe, and his two younger brothers, Arthur and Eddie. She asked me to research the tale, and I have established that something very strange did indeed take place concerning her male relatives almost a hundred years ago.

In 1908, the three brothers lived in a small street off Heyworth Street in Everton. They were George Ratcliffe, aged twenty-one, Arthur Ratcliffe, aged sixteen and fourteen-year-old Eddie. They lived with their mother and father, who was wheelchair-bound due to a degenerative disease of the spine.

One summer morning, in July 1908, the two younger Ratcliffe boys received a shilling each, a fortune for a child in those days, from a visiting aunt, and they set off to a magnificent toyshop in Victoria Street to buy a few novelties. Children grew up much more slowly in those days and played with toys for far longer than today's sophisticated computer generation. Young Edward bought a spinning top and whip, and a wind-up bird that flapped its feathered balsa wings and actually flew a short distance, and still had change left over to buy an ice cream and a soda. His brother loved jigsaw puzzles, and spent his entire shilling on a small ornamental box containing one thousand jigsaw pieces. The dark purple box was tantalisingly labelled 'One Thousand-Piece Mystery Jigsaw'.

As soon as Arthur got home, he emptied the box on to the front parlour floor and began trying to piece the puzzle together. The wooden pieces were all backed in scarlet velvet, unlike any others he had ever seen. It soon became clear that the jigsaw would be far harder to solve than the ones Arthur usually tackled, because the pieces did not seem to correspond to the picture on the box lid. However, he persevered, and by eight o'clock that night he had completed a small section of the puzzle. It was of a blonde girl whose long hair covered her naked breasts. Arthur blushed deeply when he saw the figure, and wondered what the subject of the puzzle would be when it was finished.

That evening, he was playing cricket in Stanley Park when two giggling girls approached him. One of them was blonde and her name was Alice Crosby. She looked exactly like the blonde girl in the jigsaw. Alice and Arthur started dating and she started helping him with the jigsaw. One by one, a series of images began to emerge; one showed a cloud and what looked like bank-notes raining from it, whilst another depicted a dreadful and disturbing scene – a child lying crushed under a huge cartwheel.

Two days later, a lad in Everton was running alongside a cart as it rattled over the cobbles, when he stumbled and fell under the wheels, dying instantly from multiple injuries. Arthur and Alice heard about the accident and suspected that it had not been a coincidence and were more determined than ever to complete the puzzle. They wondered what the cloud of money signified, and found out days later on the afternoon of Monday, 27 July, as they enjoyed a day out in New Brighton.

They were walking past New Brighton Tower, when suddenly, a shower of five-pound notes came fluttering down out of the sky. They eagerly snatched handsful of the money, which amounted to about sixty pounds. They thought it was a miracle, but they later discovered what had really happened from the *Liverpool Echo*. As part of a publicity campaign, the publishers of *Titbits* magazine had thrown the money off New Brighton Tower. Hundreds of their readers had cut out a special coupon which allowed them into a cordoned-off area below the tower, where they were supposed to catch the notes, but the unpredictable English weather had sabotaged the plan, and a rogue gust of wind had blown the notes away from the enclosure below the tower ... towards Arthur and Alice.

They were now more determined than ever to complete the mysterious jigsaw puzzle, but when they did so, they received a nasty shock. When the next pieces were assembled they made up a coffin, and Arthur and Alice looked at each other in trepidation. Soon afterwards, Arthur's father, who had been perfectly well, suddenly died.

Further disturbing scenes were pieced together; a figure that was unmistakably Arthur's older brother George, appeared in one scene in a military uniform. Many more scenes were assembled, including a sinking liner, motorcars, rockets, planes and horrifying images of unspeakable things. Alice became so wary of the jigsaw puzzle that she eventually refused to go anywhere near it, and stopped going round to the Ratcliffe's house.

Young Edward stepped in to help Arthur finish it, and ended up running to their mother in a state of terror. She went into the parlour to find the jigsaw virtually complete. The various scenes and events now formed a spiral, in the middle of which was a pallid, evil-looking face, which

Mrs Ratcliffe immediately took to be the Devil. Without consulting the two boys, she fetched a brush and angrily began sweeping up the pieces and shovelled them into the fire, but they wouldn't burn, despite being made of wood.

So profound was the effect of the jigsaw on the two boys that both suffered nervous breakdowns and were said to have been committed to an asylum. George Ratcliffe was killed in action in the First World War, wearing the uniform his brothers had seen him in, six years before in the jigsaw.

A STRANGE AFFAIR

A listener related the following story to me in 2003. I have had to change one or two basic details to avoid identifying the persons mentioned in the account.

In 1974, Reg, a wealthy middle-aged businessman from Gateacre, married twenty-five-year-old Audrey. People said the marriage would never work because of the twenty-five-year age difference, but Audrey and Reg seemed to be getting on very well during the first year of their marriage. Reg owned a large factory near Litherland, which was bringing in more than enough money. He had a large house in Gateacre and was planning to buy another in the country. Everything was looking rosy for him; he had a beautiful young wife, three cars and a healthy bank balance.

Things continued to go well for the newly-weds until Friday, 13 September 1974. As usual, Reg left home at 6.30am to get to the factory, kissing his wife goodbye. However, he detected a certain coldness in her kiss. She seemed to want to get it over with as quickly as possible before going back to sleep. This played on Reg's mind as he drove to the factory. He became so paranoid that he stopped the car halfway along the route and turned back home, convinced that Audrey was seeing someone else.

Determined to catch her unawares, he parked the car a short distance from the house and crept up the path, keeping to the shrubbery and out of sight of the windows. He carefully inserted his key and silently turned it – then barged in. Audrey was upstairs having a shower, so didn't hear him come in. On the coffee table in the lounge were two champagne glasses. Now Reg's suspicions were confirmed. Audrey's lipstick was on the rim of one glass, then he looked at the other, holding it carefully by the base of the stem. He could clearly see a man's thumb and fingerprint on the glass.

He stuffed the incriminating evidence into his briefcase and crept upstairs. He could see Audrey in the shower cubicle through the frosted glass. There was no one with her. Reg crept around the other rooms of the house. There was no sign of anyone hiding anywhere. Consumed with jealousy and bitterness, he listened to her singing in the shower for a moment or two, then silently left.

As he drove back to the factory, he unconsciously scowled and ground his teeth. It all made sense now – the missing cigar from his cigar box that he couldn't account for, the contraceptive pills Audrey was taking, even though she pretended to be broody. Lots of trivial little mysteries were now as clear as crystal. She was definitely seeing someone, but who it could possibly be.

There was young Terry, the young assistant manager at the factory. Reg had noticed how he had eyed Audrey when he had come round to dinner now and then, and she was always asking about him. Then there was their neighbour, Roger, the handsome bachelor who had been to their house-warming party. It had to be one of them. Audrey had virtually no social life and only moved in very small circles. Everything was done for her, everything bought and fetched. It had to be Terry or Roger.

When Reg arrived at work, he was told that Terry had called in to say that he was sick with 'flu. He raced round to his home in Fazakerley and hammered on the door. Terry answered, still in his dressing gown and looking decidedly groggy, but Reg still quizzed him about his whereabouts that morning. Terry grumpily replied, "Where do you think I've been? I've been in bed, of course. I feel awful." All the same, Reg was still suspicious and, determined to get hold of Terry's fingerprints, asked if he could use the toilet. When he was upstairs, Reg quickly grabbed a half-full glass of water from the bedside cabinet in his bedroom, emptied it down the bathroom sink, then put it in his briefcase.

He left, and immediately set off to pay a visit to an old university friend, Tony Foster, who had once been a forensic scientist at a Home Office laboratory. He asked Foster to lift the prints off the two glasses and compare them. Foster obliged, but they did not match, leaving Reg feeling even more frustrated and perplexed.

He returned home to find that Audrey had cooked him his favourite lamb casserole and bought him a box of his favourite Don Carlos Presidente cigars, as well as an ivory Prometheus cigar lighter. Reg dismissed all her efforts as transparent attempts to divert attention from the affair he was convinced she was having. Still looking for her partner in adultery, he went next door and invited his neighbour Roger to dinner. Reg did the same trick – later that night he took the wine glass from which Roger had been drinking, and took it to his friend Foster. But again he had been barking up the wrong tree – Roger's fingerprints didn't match those on the champagne glass either.

Reg now cast his net wider and acquired more and more prints from other people whom he suspected of having an affair with Audrey, still with no match. Audrey, meanwhile, remained cool and distant, which drove Reg to the verge of distraction.

One night he met an old friend and went to Liverpool city centre with him for a drink. After his friend had gone home, Reg went on a bender, and ended up in Yates's Wine Lodge near Blacklers store. He was so drunk by this time that he could hardly speak. This is where the story takes a supernatural twist. Reg suddenly collapsed and 'died'. He could hear the man who was feeling his pulse saying, "He's a gonner" and found himself in what he could later only describe as a black void. No matter which way he turned, there was nothing but infinite blackness.

At some point in this apparently timeless continuum, a figure in pale clothes appeared and knelt by him. Reg was astounded to discover that it was his brother John who had been dead for over twenty years. Reg called his name and asked where he was, and John simply said, "Eternity". Then he told Reg that he had bad news for him, he would have to go back to life again, his time had not yet come. Reg said that he didn't want to return, because he was heartbroken over Audrey's affair. John gave him a sympathetic look, then sighed, "It's the postman," and Reg hugged him with relief.

Reg woke up in hospital with Audrey squeezing his hand. As soon as he opened his eyes, his first words, "Audrey, why?" She returned a puzzled look. "It's the postman, isn't it?" he said. Audrey looked aghast, and pretended she didn't know what he was talking about, but later broke down and admitted to the affair. Reg immediately embraced her and they both sobbed – she apologising and promising never to stray again, and he forgiving her.

On the first day that he was discharged from hospital, he lay in wait for the unsuspecting postman. Behind the cover of the net curtains he watched him walk up the path towards the front door. Just as he reached the door, Reg opened it and grabbed him by the throat and threatened him. He later discovered that the man had a wife and children, which gave him even more ammunition, so he warned him that he would reveal the affair to his wife unless he stopped seeing Audrey.

That did the trick.

Somehow, Reg and Audrey fell back in love and a year later Audrey gave birth to a baby boy, who was named John, after Reg's long-dead brother.

VOICE ON THE RADIO

In November 2000, forty-year-old David Bradley, from Birkenhead, emerged from a bruising divorce feeling very depressed. He seemed to undergo a character change, becoming melancholic and telling his friends he thought life was pointless. Matthew, one of those friends, was a very spiritual person, and tried to persuade him that life was not as gloomy as he thought. Things would improve.

One evening, Matthew took David to meet a Spiritualist in Liverpool and she told him that Susan from the spirit world was very concerned about him. David was startled, because his late mother's name had been Susan. Not even Matthew had known that. David asked her to describe his mother and she did so down to the last detail. David left the

Spiritualist church a little unnerved, but a part of him wondered if it had all been a confidence trick.

In early December 2000, David descended further into depression, and one morning at three o'clock he got out of bed and decided to get into his car to drive to Nottingham. He had worked in the building trade there almost ten years before, and had dated a girl called Alexandra. She had been the most wonderful person he had ever met, but he had blown the relationship through his hard drinking – the greatest regret of his life.

When he reached his former girlfriend's home he was told that no one by the name of Alexandra lived there any more. So he drove to a cafe, and after a meal, a cup of tea and a smoke, he was back on the road, ready to return home, but had to drive through Nottingham to reach the motorway. This was on the Saturday night of 16 December 2000. He turned on his radio, and was listening to a Craig David song, 'I'm Walking Away', when all of a sudden, a familiar-sounding female voice came from that radio, interrupting the song. "David, don't turn right!" it warned.

David slowed the car, and glanced at the radio, doubting his senses. That voice had not been heard for fifteen years, yet it was unmistakably his mother, Susan Bradley's, soft gentle voice. David had intended to turn right, and he looked into his mirrors, ready to signal, but the voice came out of the radio once again, even more insistent this time. "David, don't turn right!" In that split second, he decided to obey the voice. He went straight on, but pulled over at the kerb. He sat gazing incomprehendingly at the car radio. Seeking a logical explanation for what he had heard, he checked to see if there was a tape in the cassette player. There wasn't. Trembling, he lit a cigarette and wound down the window to let in some fresh air. He felt most peculiar and suspected that he was having a nervous breakdown.

After about fifteen minutes, during which time David tried to clear his head, he became aware of a distant wailing heading in his direction. Two police cars and an ambulance rounded the bend with their sirens blaring and lights flashing. They hurtled past him and turned into the road that he was about to turn into, when his mother's voice warned him not to.

Dreading the worst, David left his car, and slowly walked towards that road. What he saw as he turned the corner was to cure him of his depression. A car had mounted the pavement at a crazy angle and from under its crumpled bonnet, crushed against a brick wall, steam was still escaping. The driver was still inside, groaning in pain. A short distance beyond the crashed car, a young man was impaled on some railings, his life rapidly ebbing away. Lying dead on the pavement nearby, was a young woman, who would subsequently be identified as the impaled man's girlfriend. It was obvious to David that her legs and arms, and probably her neck, were all broken. He stood there motionless, as the full significance of the scene sank in, until the police pushed him back up the street, away from the carnage.

As he was driving home, news of the crash came on the radio. A man in Nottingham had been out drinking with friends and had then driven home drunk. He had been travelling at fifty miles per hour in a built-up area, going the wrong way down a one-way street. The car had hit a barrier and ploughed into two Nottingham Trent students: a young man and his girlfriend. Both had been killed in the accident. The drunken driver had survived, despite crashing into the wall. He was convicted of drunken and dangerous driving and was later sent to prison for six years. Had David Bradley turned right into that one-way street, he would undoubtedly have been killed in a head-on collision.

Two months after the crash, David was visiting a friend in Southport, when he literally bumped into his old flame, Alexandra. She had hardly changed and the same emotions he had felt for her ten years ago resurfaced and were reciprocated. As he no longer drank heavily, the relationship flourished, and in July 2001, the couple were married.

David is convinced that his mother loved him so much, that she somehow managed to return from beyond the grave to save his life on that bleak Saturday night in Nottingham.

THE GHOSTLY CHARIOTEER

The subject of the following story is an apparition which I am unable to identify. Many people have encountered it over the years, although I still haven't a clue whose ghost it is, but perhaps you do, and if so, please write to me, care of my publishers (details at the end of book).

In the 1930s, the 6A tram ran from Bowring Park to the Pier Head, and this was the tram two twenty-one-year-old lads, Teddy and Bert, boarded to take them to a ball on Edge Lane. The ball continued until one in the morning, and when Teddy kissed his sweetheart from Edge Hill goodnight, he and Bert set off home on foot, as there were no trams running at that hour. The homeward journey, of over three miles, was not too arduous, since it was a warm night and they had the light of the moon to guide them, and they were both feeling merry from the wine they had consumed at the ball.

As soon as they reached the green open spaces of Bowring Park, they intended to go their separate ways, as Teddy lived in Huyton and Bert near Page Moss, but as they were saying goodnight, they heard what seemed to be the distant sound of a galloping horse. They halted and strained their ears. The horse was heading in their direction, the strangely echoing sound of its hooves steadily increasing in volume. What the two men saw next sobered them up in a flash and impressed an indelible memory on their minds.

Approaching them was the spectral figure of a woman, with long hair that billowed in the breeze as she rode a horse-drawn chariot. The phantom charioteer crossed the moonlit field at high speed, coming within thirty feet of them, before vanishing. The rattle of the chariot wheels and the thunder of galloping hooves quickly diminished, seconds after the alarming vision faded away.

Bert was so terrified that he refused to go home alone to Page Moss, the direction in which the striking apparition seemed to have been heading. He therefore stayed at Teddy's home, and throughout the rest of that night, they hardly spoke a word. Both of them had a chilling, albeit irrational conviction that the phantom charioteer had been a harbinger of death and disaster. A week later, Bert's mother died in her sleep for no apparent reason.

Not long after that, Teddy started work at Cronton Colliery, and in a freak accident, lost four fingers after getting his sleeve snagged in machinery. As he was recovering at home from his accident, a neighbour happened to mention that several people in the Huyton area had recently seen the ghost of the long-haired woman driving a chariot at breakneck speed over Bowring Park. Neither Teddy nor Bert had mentioned a word to anyone about the apparition, so that ruled out a practical joke. There were to be many more sightings of the female charioteer during the hours of darkness.

At nine o'clock on the Thursday night of Halloween, 1974, two twelve-year-old girls were crossing a field at Bowring Park, on their way home from a duck-apple party at a friend's house, when they heard the thunderous sound of galloping hooves. They grabbed each other and soon saw a horse come hurtling out of the darkness, the chariot it pulled narrowly missing them as it flew past, the wheels throwing up dirt and stones. Both girls clearly saw the woman at the reins, who was oblivious to their presence. In a repeat of her previous appearances, the phantom charioteer crossed the field at high speed.

It would seem that sightings of the magnificent ghostly charioteer of Bowring Park date back to the nineteenth century, but who she is remains a mystery.

A few years ago, what seems to have been the same ghost was seen further afield, near Speke. At the time of the sighting, the M57 was being extended and the excavations uncovered a previously unknown Roman hunting lodge, so maybe the spectral chariot dated back to Roman times.

CANNING STREET GHOST

In the Spring of 1996, Ben and Chloe, a couple from St Helen's, moved into a newly furnished flat on the second floor of a Georgian house in Canning Street in Liverpool city centre. They were the first tenants to move into the house since the premises had been renovated, and on their first night weird things began to happen. A very sweet scent pervaded the living room around midnight, and the sounds of someone walking slowly up the stairs from the bottom flight to the top could be heard. Ben was so sure that an intruder was outside the door, that he shouted, "Who's there?" And in reply, something rapped three times on the door. When he opened it, no one was there.

One night, about a week later, Chloe was sitting in bed reading by the light of a bedside lamp, when an incident occurred which almost paralysed her with fear. The tall black figure of a man stepped right out of the solid wall by her bed. He wore a top hat and a long cape, but although his shirt and collar were white, his neck, face and hands were as black and featureless as a silhouette. He picked up the glass of water from the bedside cabinet, lifted it to the ovoid blackness of his face, took a sip, then put it back. He then turned so swiftly that his cape swirled in a semi-circle behind him, and melted back into the wall.

When Ben returned home from work at nine o'clock, he found Chloe standing outside on the steps, in great distress. It took him a long time to persuade her to go back into their flat. When she showed him the drinking glass from which the ghost had sipped, she let out a yelp of revulsion and slammed it back down on the cabinet as though it were alive. On the rim was a silvery, sticky residue, as fine as a cobweb. Ben later took the glass to be examined by two university students studying parapsychology. They intended to have the weird substance analysed but the specimen had somehow evaporated from its sealed container before they could get it to a laboratory. A fortnight later, the so-called parapsychologists ran yelling from the flat after a freezing invisible hand had stroked their faces.

One Friday night, Chloe intended to go out on the town with several work-mates, but refused to shower unless one of her friends stood guard outside the cubicle. Her friend Sam laughingly agreed to keep watch and sat reading a magazine. Some time later, Chloe heard a loud bump, so she switched off the shower, wiped the water from her eyes, and through the frosted glass made out someone in black standing there. It was unmistakably the outline of the top-hatted ghost. She screamed at the top of her voice, and the figure vanished. When she ventured outside the shower unit, she found the door wide open. Her friend had also seen the ghost, and had been rendered speechless and had charged straight out of the house. Sam never returned to that apartment and still refuses to go anywhere near Canning Street. However, there were two more terrifying incidents still to come.

Just under a month later, Chloe and Ben were in bed one night, when he went to fetch a snack from the kitchen. Chloe relaxed back and yawned. She stretched up her arms and yawned again and as she did so, a pair of icy hands shot out from behind the headboard and seized her tightly by the wrists. When she looked up, she saw the same ink black shadow of a face looming over her. This time she was so petrified she lost consciousness. When she came round, she was on the sofa in the living room and Ben was leaning over her saying this was the final straw. They were leaving. They could spend the night in his uncle's in Crosby. At three in the morning, the couple snatched up a few possessions, climbed into their brand new car and drove off.

As the car was speeding down Parliament Street, they became aware of the same sweet scent that had pervaded their apartment just before all the supernatural trouble had started. The driving-wheel in Ben's hands suddenly swung left all by itself, as if someone with superhuman strength was yanking it. The car veered left and mounted the kerb on the corner of Windsor Street. Ben somehow managed to regain control of the vehicle, and luckily no pedestrians were about at that hour. Shaken, but back in control, he continued down Chaloner Street towards Wapping, when once again something very powerful spun the steering wheel sharply left. This time, the car swerved violently down a road past the Salthouse Dock. The accelerator pedal was being pressed down by an invisible force, and even though Ben had taken his foot off the clutch, the car refused to stall.

The car was about to hurtle down the sloping ramp into the dock itself, when Ben yanked on the handbrake in a last-ditch attempt to stop it, and the possessed car screeched, turned through 180 degrees, and eventually stopped dead. Ben told Chloe to leave the car and stand well out of harm's way, and he drove it to a car park and abandoned it. He and Chloe then hailed a taxi which took them to Crosby, but even in the taxi, the malevolent spirit would not give in. It swerved violently, and the cabby apologised, saying the steering seemed to be wonky, even though he knew for a fact that there was nothing wrong with the vehicle.

Ben and Chloe still can't understand why the malicious ghost chose to victimise them, but I have heard many other accounts of the Canning Street ghost which haunts their former address. My theory is that the spirit is that of some stern Victorian gentleman who resents people living in what he considers to be his old house.

JOURNEYS OF THE MIND

One miserable night in February 1950, Alf, a quiet inoffensive man of about seventy, was having supper in the old Sailors' Home in Liverpool. For years he had told anyone who cared to listen of his adventures at sea in the regular Navy and the Merchant Navy, and most of his listeners had assumed that he was telling the truth.

However, on this particular night, a man named George, who had spent most of his life at sea, confronted Alf over one of his claims. He had mentioned that he had served on the *Empress of India* under Admiral Beattie, but George had served on that same ship, and had no recollection of Alf being onboard. For a while, Alf persisted in his claim, but was finally forced to admit that he had lied. He had never served in either the British Navy, or the Merchant Navy, because all his life he had suffered from epilepsy, and no naval service would take him. His illness had made life very difficult for a man who had come from a seafaring family, which could claim ancestors in Nelson's Navy.

Back in 1860, the Sailors' Home on Canning Street had caught fire and several men were trapped in the building's upper floors. They leaned out of the windows, crying out for help, but when a ladder was raised to rescue them, it was found to be too short. A brave young sailor in the crowd rushed up the ladder, despite the cries of the police urging him to come back down. He was William, Alf's father. He stood on the very top rung and gripped the window ledge. "Come on!" he cried to the men, who were now choking from the smoke and fumes billowing out of the window.

One by one, the men climbed out and scrambled over the sailor's body and on to the ladder. Then William cried out as a wall of flames suddenly shot up from the window below and burnt his legs and face, scarring him for life. All the same, he managed to get back down without help, and was hailed as the hero.

Twenty years later, in 1880, Alf was born, William's ninth son. Every other son had gone into the Navy, or served on a ship, but Alf began having fits when he was ten and it soon became clear that he would never go to sea, even though it was in his blood. Alf's father virtually disowned him, ashamed to have a son who couldn't follow in his footsteps. As well as listening to his father and his brothers, he had learned about the sea from books. He knew every naval battle, every maritime disaster, and related vivid accounts of them as if he had been there in person, yet in reality, he had never even ventured as far as the Isle of Man.

The sailors in the home were amazed when they found out the truth about Alf, and many of them felt conned and quite foolish. In particular, they thought about Alf's gripping tales as first mate aboard the *Washington Queen*. Each night, over cocoa and rum, Alf would spin a salty yarn about his adventures on that the ship, and how he had roamed the seven seas on her. Had all that been a tissue of lies as well? they asked him. Alf tearfully insisted that there really was a ship called the *Washington Queen*. He even claimed it was his own ship, but no one believed him now and one by one, each sailor turned his back on him. No one told the old man to go, but he felt so ashamed at being caught out and branded a liar, that he packed his few belongings, and left the Sailors' Home just after midnight.

Feeling utterly miserable and dejected, he wandered through the freezing February night, down the frigid, deserted city streets, towards the old landing stage at the Pier Head, perhaps to reflect on a life that he had yearned for, but which had been denied him by a cruel affliction. That was where he was last seen alive, for on the following morning, a group of children came upon Alf's cold, stiff body in Shaw Street Park, lying huddled up inside a wooden longboat in a sandpit. He was covered by a skimpy layer of crumpled newspapers, and a post-mortem established that he had died from hypothermia.

One of Alf's friends later visited the park to see the place where he had died and to pay his respects. He went to the children's play area and came upon the wooden longboat in the sandpit. As he drew near, he suddenly noticed the words *Washington Queen* scrawled in faded paint along the side of the land-locked boat, and realised with a start, that he was looking at the ship that had taken Alf on so many seafaring journeys of the imagination.

It was said that not long after Alf's death, his ghost was often seen in Shaw Street Park, smiling fondly at groups of children playing at being sailors in the old wooden boat.

THE MESSAGE

In the early 1990s, Amy, an ambitious twenty-year-old from Kirkby, decided to apply for a job in America as a proof-reader and sub editor with a magazine based in Greenwich Village, New York. Everyone said she stood no chance of getting the job, but the letter she sent to the company was regarded as being so original and honest, that she was invited over to New York to work for a trial period. She got on so well that she ended up being employed at the publishing house and later obtained a green card. She married a New Yorker in 1995, but ended up divorced through irreconcilable differences by the year 2000.

In the year 2001, on Valentine's Day, Amy was alone in her Manhattan apartment. She couldn't help thinking about her failed marriage and how lonely she now was, and she became more and more miserable. Her doorbell sounded, and when she answered, it was David, a work colleague. David was only five foot three, rather plump, balding and wore thick-lensed spectacles. In his arms he held a massive bouquet of red roses. Amy's face lit up when she saw him standing there with the roses, and she was just about to thank him for the Valentine gesture when he said, "Er ...I found these down here at your door."

"Really?" Amy examined the roses, but there was no little note, no indication as to who had sent them. She looked up and down the corridor, baffled.

"Another admirer, obviously," said David, as he walked into the apartment. Amy was intrigued by the roses, and sat drinking wine that evening, speculating on the identity of her secret admirer. She suspected and hoped that it was the man who worked as a bartender at a wine bar she often visited after work with her friends. His name was Matt. Throughout the evening Amy talked about Matt's sense of humour, how wide his shoulders were and his cute lop-sided smile. At one point in her ramblings, something suddenly occurred to her and she asked David, "Hey, you didn't leave those roses at my door did you ...?"

"Ha! No, I did not," said David, avoiding eye contact with her. "I'd never do anything as cheesy as that."

Amy jokingly replied, "... because if you did, you'd be wasting your time. You're the best friend a person could have, but you know the type of man I go for."

"Yes ... I know ... I'm not anyone's type of guy," sighed David resignedly. After a pensive few moments he added, "I wish people could see the inside of a person, instead of just the thin outer layer," and in a barely audible voice added, "there's so much love in my soul." Embarrassed at having revealed his true feelings, he made some excuse and left.

On the following day, Amy walked into the wine bar after work, and made a remark to Matt about some anonymous admirer leaving her a bouquet of roses. Matt smiled, exuding his usual charm. After a few glasses of wine, Amy asked if he had left the flowers. She had to know.

"Maybe," said Matt.

That night, Matt went back to Amy's apartment and stayed the night. It was the beginning of an intense and passionate affair, which lasted until August – when Amy discovered that he was married with two lovely young daughters. She found out in the worst possible way; she was walking hand in hand with him one morning down Fifth Avenue, when they bumped into the children's mother. Matt's wife gave him a choice there and then – Amy or her. Matt chose his wife, and left Amy standing there alone, crushed and humiliated. The end of the affair had a devastating effect on her and now, after work, she avoided going out and became a virtual recluse.

One unbearable Tuesday morning, a few weeks after being ditched by Matt, Amy decided to call work and say she was sick. She left a message on her boss's answering machine, swallowed a sleeping pill and curled up in bed feeling sorry for herself. She wished that David was there to share her troubles, but he had started a new job in Manhattan. Suddenly, at around a quarter to nine, she saw David's kind, bespectacled face looking at her as she drifted into a dream. He was smiling affectionately, and suddenly, in the dream, she fell in love with him. She realised what he had said about people never looking at the beauty and love within a person, just the skin-deep shallow beauty.

Amy woke up with her heart pounding, and felt as if she was in love for the first time in her life. She went to call David, but noticed that she had a text message on her cell phone. She felt dizzy as she read it: 'Amy, I love you, and always will love you. I left the roses at your door. I can tell you now, because it doesn't matter anymore. Love, David.'

Still holding the phone and wondering what the last line meant, Amy groggily sat down and switched on the television. On the CNN channel the almost unbelievable images of the stricken World Trade Center were being broadcast – the Twin Towers engulfed in flames and billowing vast clouds of thick black smoke. Amy remembered that David had just started his new job there and frantically tried to call him, but an automated voice stated that his phone could not be reached.

Amy later discovered that David had perished in the terrorist attacks on the Twin Towers. He had been on the one hundred and seventh floor. Like so many other victims who knew they were about to die, he had sent a text message to the person he loved most in the world. Many heartbreaking telephone calls were made from the towers that morning. David had probably been afraid of rejection, because he imagined he was unattractive, but felt he had nothing to lose by declaring his love for Amy in the last moments of his life.

On Valentine's Day, 2002, Amy received a mysterious text message which read, 'Love never dies'. It could not be traced. She knows in her heart that it was from David.

I See a Dark Stranger

Madame Rosalind De Vere was a fortune-teller who was also known by many other names in the Liverpool of the forties, fifties and sixties. She had once called herself Madame Zodia during one 'incarnation'.

One lunchtime, in the summer of 1966, nineteen-year-old Nancy Fenn left Blacklers, the store where she worked, and instead of going to the kiosk to buy cigarettes and crisps, as she usually did, she went with her friend Violet, to Madame De Vere's parlour, in the Bold Street area. Nancy had heard a lot about her amazing predictions, which included the foretelling of her older sister's pregnancy. She had even forecast that she would have twins.

Nancy and Violet climbed the stairs until they reached the dark room over the shop. Nancy sat at a small round table draped with a purple cloth facing Madame De Vere, who was staring directly into her shy blue eyes. The self-conscious girl's eyelashes fluttered. She took half a crown from her purse and handed it to the old woman, and soon the prediction was delivered, though no palms were read, nor crystal balls consulted.

"I see a dark stranger," began Madame De Vere.

Violet giggled in the darkness somewhere in background.

"Shh," hissed Nancy under her breath.

The fortune-teller continued, "He is very tall and very handsome, but beware, my dear, beware! He will come into your life on a Thursday, the last day of this month."

"Why did you say 'beware'? Can you tell me any more?"

"There's a shadow over him and that usually portends evil or vice. I am unable to penetrate that shadow, because it is so dark."

Violet giggled again, and the fortune-teller ordered the girls to leave. The smile was wiped from Violet's face when Madame De Vere called after her, "You won't have much to smile about next week."

The remark left her feeling very edgy. When she got home her mum was holding a letter. "Violet, this is from the hospital. They've set a date next week for you to have your tonsils out."

Violet felt faint, and said, "No, I'm fine, Mam. I don't think I need it anymore."

But her mother insisted. She had suffered recurrent bouts of tonsillitis for years and had waited over eighteen months for the operation. Fortunately, the tonsillectomy was a success, but shortly after the operation Violet had awakened in pain to find nurses with what appeared to be toothbrushes, frantically rubbing away huge, solid clots in her throat that had formed from unexpected haemorrhaging.

Nancy, meanwhile, waited for the last day of June, which was a Thursday. On that date, a tall, dark-haired man of about thirty walked into Blacklers. He spoke with a slight Cockney accent, and after she had served him at the till, he remarked on her good looks. He seemed charming, and really did have a genuine twinkle in his eye when he looked at Nancy, who felt herself colour under his gaze. He was holding up a queue of grumbling shoppers, so he walked away, lurked about for a while, then returned. His name was Joe Hughes, and he was staying at the YMCA. He was very forward and asked her name. Peeping shyly from beneath her fringe, she told him it was Nancy.

"Okay, Nancy with the laughing face, I'm going to make a fool of myself now. I'm going to ask you out, because if I don't, I'll regret it for the rest of my life."

Nancy felt hot all over, especially when she noticed a

young lad who worked at the store listening in. That boy, Frankie, also liked Nancy, so to impress him, she decided to accept Joe's romantic offer. Joe Hughes kissed her knuckles and told her to meet him at the YMCA at 7.30pm that night. Then he left. Frankie was gutted, and told Nancy that the man looked far too old for her. She ignored him, dreamily saying that Joe's eyes were lovely.

That night, Nancy went to the YMCA on Mount Pleasant and found Joe waiting for her, dressed in the height of fashion. He took her to the Beehive, then on to a nearby club. Throughout the evening he behaved like a true gentleman and even paid for a taxi to take her home to Everton, which really impressed her parents. Two weeks later, in his basement flat on Catherine Street, he and Nancy were sitting close together on a sofa when she asked, "What d'you think is the most attractive part of me? I mean face-wise? Is it my eyes? People seem to think so."

Joe nodded, adding, "And your neck!" And he put his hand around her neck and smiled. Something in that smile, and in the way he grasped her neck, made her feel very uncomfortable and she pushed him away.

The next day, Nancy dragged Joe to Bold Street, to visit the fortune-teller once more, eager to know if she would be married, have children, and so on. Joe thought it a complete waste of time and said so, but went along anyway. They sat before Madame De Vere, who seemed to be studying Joe intently. She read the couple's future, then said, "Nancy, I see you wearing his ..." and the fortune-teller seemed to lose her voice.

"You see me wearing his what?" asked Nancy. "His ring?"

Madame De Vere gasped and said, "I see you wearing his ... tie. It's tight round your neck ... tight ... choking you!"

Nancy shook her head and turned to Joe, expecting him

to see the whole thing as a joke. The look of pure evil on his face chilled her. In a rage, he stood up and pointed a finger at the fortune-teller's face, "I'll come back for you!" he spat, then swung round and left. Nancy rose to follow him, but the old woman held her back saying, "No, don't go after him, he's a murderer," then led her into the safety of the room next door and firmly locked it. She told her that in the vision she had seen him strangling women and dumping them in a river.

Love is blind, and Nancy chose to ignore her dire warning. A short time later she called at the Catherine Street flat to see her beloved Joe, but he was gone, along with all his belongings.

At that time, there was a serial killer at large in London nicknamed Jack the Stripper, who dumped the naked bodies of his victims in the River Thames. Some had been strangled with a tie, and even their own undergarments. Some thought the killer was the boxer, Freddie Mills, others that he was a policeman, but he was never caught. There were also many rumours that the killer had fled the capital and gone north. Was Nancy's handsome boyfriend the London serial-killer? And had she been saved from his murderous clutches by the old fortune-teller?